AQA English Literature B

AS

Exclusively endorsed by AQA

Adrian Beard
Dr Alan Kent

Nelson Thornes

Published in 2008 by:
Nelson Thornes Ltd
Delta Place
27 Bath Road
CHELTENHAM
GL53 7TH
United Kingdom

09 10 11 12 / 10 9 8 7 6 5 4 3

A catalogue record for this book is available from the British Library

ISBN 978 0 7487 8288 8

Cover photograph by Photolibrary
Illustrations by Dave Eaton
Page make-up by Pantek Arts Ltd, Maidstone, Kent

Printed in China by 1010 Printing International Ltd.

The authors and publishers wish to thank the following for permission to use copyright
material:

Caters News Agency for extracts from Charlotte Dalton, 'He Died a Hero', *Woman's Own*,
30.10.06; Faber and Faber Ltd for W H Auden, 'Oh What is that Sound' from Collected
Poems by *W H Auden* (1991); David Higham Associates on behalf of the translator for
material from Henrik Ibsen, *Hedda Gabler* from *Plays Two*, trs. Michael Meyer, Methuen
Drama (1985) pp. 254–7; Random House Group Ltd for Robert Frost, 'The Road Less
Travelled' from *The Poetry of Robert Frost*, Chatto & Windus; for extracts from Ian McEwan,
Enduring Love, Jonathan Cape (1997) pp. 1–3. 55–6. Copyright © 1997 Ian McEwan; and
Anne Tyler, *Digging to America*, Chatto & Windus (2006) pp. 4–5, 22–3; Rogers, Coleridge
& White Ltd on behalf of the author for extracts from Richard Ford, *A Multitude of Sins*,
Vintage Books (1996) pp. 290–1. Copyright © Richard Ford 1996; The Wylie Agency,
Inc on behalf of the author for extracts from Arthur Miller, *Death of a Salesman* (1949).
Copyright © 1977 by Arthur Miller;

Every effort has been made to trace the copyright holders but if any have been
inadvertently overlooked the publishers will be pleased to make the necessary
arrangement at the first opportunity.

p.15 © Craig Lovell/Corbis; p.29 © The Bridgeman Art Library; p.61 © Swim Ink 2, LLC/
Corbis; p.69 20th Century Fox/Paramount/The Kobal Collection; p.70 © New Line/Everett/
Rex Features; p.81 © Everett Collection/Rex Features; p81 © Corbis Sygma; p.96 ©
Robbie Jack/Corbis; p.89 © Joe Cocks Studio Collection © Shakespeare Birthplace Trust
(1987 production); p.91 Angus McBean © Royal Shakespear Company (1955 production);
p.105 © B. Rafferty/Lebrecht Music & Ar; p.110 © Robbie Jack/Corbis; p.116 Alastair
Muir/Rex Features

Contents

AQA introduction

Nelson Thornes has worked in partnership with AQA to ensure this book and the accompanying online resources offer you the best support for your GCSE course.

All resources have been approved by senior AQA examiners so you can feel assured that they closely match the specification for this subject and provide you with everything you need to prepare successfully for your exams.

These print and online resources together **unlock blended learning**; this means that the links between the activities in the book and the activities online blend together to maximise your understanding of a topic and help you achieve your potential.

These online resources are available on **kerboodle!** which can be accessed via the internet at **http://www.kerboodle.com/live**, anytime, anywhere. If your school or college subscribes to this service you will be provided with your own personal login details. Once logged in, access your course and locate the required activity.

For more information and help visit **http://www.kerboodle.com**

Icons in this book indicate where there is material online related to that topic. The following icons are used:

Learning activity

These resources include a variety of interactive and non-interactive activities to support your learning.

Progress tracking

These resources enable you to analyse and understand examination questions (On your marks...).

Research support

These resources include WebQuests, in which you are assigned a task and provided with a range of web links to use as source material for research.

Study skills

These resources support you as you develop a skill that is key for your course, for example planning essays.

Analysis tool

These resources help you to analyse key texts and images by providing questions and prompts to focus your response.

How to use this book

This book covers the specification for your course and is arranged in a sequence approved by AQA. The introduction to the book explains what will be required of you as an English Literature student. There are two units in the book, Unit 1 will prepare you for the examination. This unit deals with various aspects of narrative that you may choose to write about in your answers. Chapter 7 draws these aspects together to show how you might construct a response for the examination which covers all of these aspects, whilst Chapter eight deals specifically with preparation for the exam itself.

Unit 2 is a guide to your coursework study, based on a study of aspects of tragedy. This unit takes you through tragic conventions, concepts and theories from Ancient Greek tragedy to modern domestic tragedy, using key extracts from Shakespeare and other playwrights. Chapter 16 explains in detail how to prepare for, write and create a commentary on your coursework.

Definitions of any words that appear in bold can be found in the glossary at the back of this book.

Definitions of any words that appear in bold can be found in the glossary at the back of this book.

Learning objectives

At the beginning of each section you will find a list of learning objectives that contain targets linked to the requirements of the specification.

The features in this book include:

Key terms

Terms that you will need to be able to define and understand. These terms are coloured blue in the text book and their definition will also appear in the glossary at the back of this book.

Hint

Useful suggestions for study.

Remember

Reminder of key terms and ideas that you have already come across earlier in the text book.

Links

Links to other areas in the text book which are relevant to what you are reading. Links can also refer you to longer extracts to be used in activities; these can be found in the Extracts section at the back of the book.

Further reading

Suggestions for other texts that will help you in your study and preparation for assessment in English Literature B.

Activity

Activities which develop the skills you will need for success in your English Literature B course.

Extension tasks

Tasks which take your learning further to increase your skills and give you even more knowledge and understanding, preparing you to demonstrate capabilities worthy of high grades. You should complete these activities when you have extra time after completing the activities.

Commentaries

Examples of answers you might give to the activities. These are designed to help you to understand what type of response the examiner is looking for. Commentaries sometimes appear directly after the activity and sometimes at the end of the chapter in the section headed Commentaries.

Did you know?

Interesting facts to extend your background knowledge.

 Examiner's tip

Hints from AQA examiners to help you with your study and to prepare for your exam.

Summary

A summary of what is covered in this chapter of the book.

AQA examination questions are reproduced by permission of the Assessment and Qualifications Alliance.

Introduction to this book

Aims of the chapter:

■ Presents your AS Level English Literature course.

■ Explains how your work for each of the two units of the course will be assessed.

Welcome to AS Level English Literature. It is worth reading this first chapter at the start of your course, when it will give you some ideas about what is to come, and then you can return to it when you have had more experience of reading your texts and working with this book.

The course at a glance

AS Level English Literature has two units: Unit 1 is taken as a formal exam; Unit 2 is coursework. How the work is divided up in terms of time, and among your teachers, will depend very much on the circumstances in the institution you attend – so you could prepare for Unit 1 first and then do Unit 2, or you could prepare for them both simultaneously, or you could do them in reverse numerical order.

It is always worth remembering that across the course as a whole you will do much more reading and preparation than the exam/coursework can possibly assess. This means that the assessment is a snapshot of what you have been doing, rather than the whole process. As we move on to look at how the assessment works, try to see it as a shaping mechanism rather than the be-all and end-all of what AS Level English Literature is all about.

Unit 1: Aspects of Narrative

The full implication of this unit's title will be explained in the next chapter. In outline, though, you will do the following in preparation for this unit:

■ you will read and study two novels from a set text list

■ you will read and study two poetry texts from a set text list.

You can take all four texts into the exam with you, but you are not allowed to make any annotations in them beforehand. In many cases the overall poetry 'text' is made up of a number of separate poems.

The box below outlines the ways in which Unit 1 will be assessed.

Assessment of Unit 1: Aspects of Narrative

Exam: 2 hours (open-book)
60% of total AS marks
30% of total A Level marks

Four texts for study:
Two novels (at least one post-1990)
Two poetry texts (1800–1945)

Two sections, one question to be answered from each section:

Section A

■ Involves close analysis of narrative method in **one** text

■ Contains specific questions on each of the set texts

■ One two-part question to be answered on your chosen text

■ Short answer required for each of the two parts

Section B

■ Involves comparing an aspect of narrative across **three** texts

■ Contains two questions, wide-ranging in scope

■ Essay required on the three texts you have not covered in Section A

Unit 2: Dramatic Genres

The **genre** referred to in the unit's title is *Tragedy*. The full implication of this unit will be explained later in the book. In outline, though, you will do the following in preparation for this unit:

■ you will read and study a Shakespeare play that can be labelled a tragedy

■ you will read and study another play which can also be labelled a tragedy.

After you have studied the texts, you will produce a portfolio of coursework consisting of two written responses, one on each text. In each piece of work

Key terms

Genre: a type of text (e.g. a crime novel, a narrative poem). Texts can be grouped and labelled for various reasons, such as their content, their intended audience (e.g. a children's novel), how readers respond to them, etc.

your response will involve thinking about the play within the broader generic frameworks of drama and tragedy.

In this unit there is also the possibility of writing what is sometimes called a **re-creative response**. If you intend to use this method, you will need to negotiate the task carefully with your tutor. You also need to provide a commentary to go with the response, in which you can explain the thinking behind your approach, and what it has shown you about the original text.

Key terms

Re-creative response: a piece of writing which throws light on the original text in a creative rather than an analytical way.

The box below outlines the ways in which Unit 2 will be assessed.

Assessment of Unit 2: Dramatic Genres (Aspects of Tragedy)

Coursework
40% of total AS marks
20% of total A Level marks

Minimum **two** texts for study within dramatic genre of tragedy
A portfolio of **two** pieces of written coursework (one may be re-creative), **1200–1500 words** for each piece:

1   An aspect of dramatic/tragic genre with regard to a Shakespeare play
2   An aspect of dramatic/tragic genre with regard to another play

---

Assessment Objectives

As part of the process by which all specifications are regulated, English Literature is broken down into four Assessment Objectives, or AOs as they are commonly called.

These AOs do not specify the content of your course as such, but they do specify the skills and approaches that you are required to cover. As a student you do not need to worry about covering them, provided you answer the question, whether it be an exam or coursework. The question will be designed to cover the skills and approaches – your job is to answer its requirements exactly.

None the less it is useful for you to have an understanding of what these AOs actually say. The box in the margin gives them in their official format. But what are their implications in more practical terms?

AO1
Articulate, creative, informed and relevant responses to literary texts, using appropriate terminology and concepts, and coherent, accurate written expression

AO2
Demonstrate detailed critical understanding in analysing the ways in which structure, form and language shape meanings in literary texts

AO3
Explore connections and comparisons between different literary texts, informed by interpretations of other readers

AO4
Demonstrate understanding of the significance and influence of the contexts in which literary texts are written and received

---

AO1

Two key elements combine here: the quality of your writing and your knowledge of the necessary terminology that goes with this subject. All AS Level subjects have their own specialist language and their own academic conventions when it comes to writing. The specialist terminology that you need will emerge as you go through the book and can be checked in the glossary at the end of the book.

Below are some of the types of writing you could come across during your AS course:

* short answers, which require no introduction or conclusion
* essays in exams, but with text available
* a coursework essay
* a piece of re-creative writing.

Each of these is subtly different, but each needs to be practised and improved. English Literature is all about reading, but it is assessed totally by writing. You therefore need to prepare for your AS assessments by working at your writing skills, making sure that you know exactly what is required.

AO2

This is concerned with how texts work, how they are constructed – what authors do with language when they write. The best order in which to take the three key terms is as follows: **form**, **structure**, **language** – that is, the biggest unit first and the smallest last.

Key terms

Form: the aspects of a text in its totality that enable it to be identified as a novel, or a poem, or an epistolary novel (i.e. a story told in the form of letters) or a sonnet (a poem of 14 lines), etc.

Structure: how the significant parts of a text work together to form a whole (e.g. the connection between chapters in a novel, or the way time is organised, or the connection between verses in a poem).

Language: in this context, generally refers to specific words or phrases in the text.

Of the three terms, looking at the use of language in a text can be useful in poetry, but it tends to have less significance in novels and plays.

As you work through this book you will acquire considerable expertise in how to analyse texts in order to meet the requirements of AO2.

AO3

AO3 has two parts to it. It requires that you make connections and comparisons across texts and that when you make these connections you are aware that you are not dealing with absolutes – there are other ways in which the texts can be interpreted, in which case different connections might be made.

At the heart of this idea of interpreting texts through connecting them with others is the idea of **genre**, or type of text. Generic labels help us to identify what a text is like, but we need to be aware that although it has some qualities in common with the other texts it may also be different from them.

In this AO, then, we look for similarity and difference across the texts we are studying, and we will probably find people disagreeing about whether various categories apply. This means that when we are studying literature we are not dealing with fixed and known interpretations.

AO4

AO4 follows naturally from AO3, because how you categorise a text depends on various factors, or **contexts**, which shape your response. Contexts can arise from circumstances to do with the way the text was produced, sometimes called **contexts of production**, and contexts to do with the way it is received now, sometimes called **contexts of reception**.

Key terms

Context: the circumstances surrounding a text (e.g. where it first appeared, social attitudes today) which affect the way it is understood. The word is formed from *con* (= with) + *text*, so literally it means 'what goes with the text'.

Being aware of the context of a text, and its interpretation, is always important, but if you are not careful you can allow context to become more important than the text itself. That is why this course tends to focus rather more on contexts of reception: you are unlikely in this specification to be asked specifically about historical contexts, although they may of course be referred to when relevant.

 Examiner's tip

You have heard it stated many times, but the key to doing well in your exam is answering the question exactly as it is worded. It is the examiners' job to make sure all the technical requirements of the course are met through the questions. It is your job to do exactly as the question states – no more, no less!

Summary

This introduction has outlined the content of the course and the way in which it will be assessed, and has raised some issues regarding the course overall. You will find it useful to refer back to it occasionally to keep yourself informed of the overall design of the course.

1 Aspects of Narrative

Introduction to Unit 1

Aims of the chapter:

- Introduces Unit 1, Aspects of Narrative.

- Considers some of your workload requirements.

- Gives answers to some of the key questions you are likely to face as you start the course.

Reading the texts

A couple of points should almost go without saying: you cannot study literature if you have not read the books, and ways of reading the books differ considerably. So novels need to be read privately, and then discussed in class with reference to key passages. Poems, on the other hand, need to be both read and heard, and are much more amenable to collaborative working throughout.

Reading and studying the novels

When we read for pleasure (and millions do – it is an ever growing pastime) most of us read with various levels of intensity and with enough sense of recall for us to get to the end without having to keep stopping to remember who people are and what they did earlier. We then move on to the next novel and our short-term memory quickly fades.

Studying a novel is different. Its very length means that it cannot be returned to endlessly, yet you are required to have a very good knowledge of the text so that you can access it very quickly in an exam. (The fact that the exam is open-book makes no difference here. The open-book exam allows the examiner to set specific questions on chapters of novels, but you do not have time then to actually read the chapter – a skim reading and recognition of its key features is all you will have time for.)

Your knowledge of the book also has to be such that you can discuss aspects of it in any chronological order – if Chapter 14 is the most relevant, and it connects in various ways with Chapter 8, then you need to be able to make the links and sift the novel to pick out relevant sections.

How then should you read the set-text novels? The following are some common questions and answers.

How many times should I read the novels?

It would be easy to come up with a high figure, but the reality is that you have lots of reading to do, and not just in this subject. The minimum would be once through before you start studying the novel in class and once as you prepare for the exam – at other times you will be accessing parts of the novel and rereading them. When you are reading and working through this textbook, you will find frequent points when you are asked to go back to your novels for evidence of a particular point that is being made. The advantage of working in a class or group is that the burden of this, and other work, can be shared.

Of the two novels you are studying, you might focus on one in more detail than the other.

Do I need to read the novels before we start studying them in class?

Absolutely. If you are 'reading as you go' you will never see the whole text, and you will inevitably force your teacher into the chapter-by-chapter approach, which is not very helpful to your learning.

Do I just read the novels, or do I make notes?

This in part depends on how many times you intend to read the novels. If you think you can only manage to read them twice, then you need to make the most of each reading. Certainly at some point you will need to come up with a chapter-by-chapter synopsis – or use one provided by somebody else. Again tasks can be shared across a class or group. Typically a group might share the following tasks and present them to the class – you are then in a position to add your own details when it comes to revision:

- a synopsis of each chapter
- a 'tree' of how characters and actions connect
- a 'map' of various locations and settings
- a timeline of key events and where they are placed in the novel.

Reading and studying the poetry

Depending on the choices that are made from within the selected set texts, the word 'poetry' will have a slightly different meaning. Sometimes the poetry counting as a set text will consist of several poems by the same author. In other cases it will be fewer but longer poems, and in one or two cases it might even be a single long poem.

Clearly the ways in which we read and study poems differ from the ways we read and study novels. Poems have both a visual and an aural dimension: they can be read silently and privately, but they can also be heard publicly. When you study the poems it is likely that you will do so in a group or class context, with the poems being heard. Private revision, on the other hand, requires you to 'hear' the poems in your head if you are to fully appreciate how they work.

Reading poetry aloud does not come naturally to many, and indeed some poetry readings can sound very artificial. (Strangely, sometimes the very worst readers are the poets themselves.) Even if you are not that good at reading aloud, you really ought to try to work at reading these poems aloud, because by doing so you will be forced to find meanings in them. This requires help, patience, practice and confidence. The end result of this, though, is that when you turn to a poem in the exam, you not only see it, you also hear it in your head, and by hearing it you make meanings.

How then should you read the set-text poetry? The following are some common questions and answers.

Do I need to read the poems before we start studying them in class?

It always helps to have some prior knowledge, but in this instance much of the reading will also be done in class.

How many times should I read the poems?

Obviously it takes less time to read the poems, but their meanings and techniques tend to be much more condensed. You will therefore need to read them several times to explore and understand them. Each time you read them you will be looking for something specific: the ways in which people are presented, for example, or the different voices that the poem contains.

AQA Examiner's tip

When you write about the novels, remember that:

- your markers have read them, but not quite as closely as you have
- they are interested in your arguments but need you to prove them
- they need reminding of key moments rather than being told about them in detail.

Hint

Reading poems aloud helps you to 'hear' as well as 'see' them, and so helps you to understand and appreciate them more fully than if you only read them silently.

Remember

Every time you read a set text, you do so with a research purpose in mind: you are looking for specific meanings or techniques.

What is special about poetry?

As mentioned above, poetry is a condensed form of expression with many more patterns to it than prose fiction. These patterns can include:

- repetition of structure (e.g. verses)
- repetition of metaphorical language (e.g. imagery and symbolism)
- repetition of sound (e.g. rhyme and rhythm)
- repetition of voice (e.g. speakers identified by certain speech habits).

The poems you are studying have been selected because in various ways they provide examples of narratives – they tell stories. The mixture of condensed language and patterning, though, means that these stories need to be uncovered by close reading strategies, sometimes closer than those that apply to novels.

Do I just read the poems, or do I make notes?

You definitely make notes, but as always be selective in what you write down, focusing on the key issues of narrative rather than on what could be incidental detail.

Should I learn quotations?

Because this is an open-book exam, you will have the texts in front of you. This means that you may not need to commit so much to memory, but you will need to know where to find the right quotation without delay. So it is probably worth knowing some key quotations, but you also need to know how to navigate your way around the poems quickly.

Link

See Chapter 2 for an explanation of metaphorical language and symbolism.

Examiner's tip

It is possible to read the set texts endlessly and convince yourself that you are doing quality revision. In fact, though, you need to do more than this: you need to reread the texts with research questions in mind, making notes as you go. Reading on its own will not achieve much; reading with a purpose will achieve much more. Many students have found it useful to keep an exercise book for notes on each of their texts. You could also keep your own computer-based notes.

Summary

This chapter has introduced you to some key features of Unit 1 and looked at some of the most important questions which arise when preparing for your study of the texts themselves.

1 Introducing narrative

- ■ Presents some key terms to do with narrative.

- ■ Explains that stories are representations of the world, not the world itself.

- ■ Describes the key aspects of narrative.

Unit 1 of your AS course is entitled 'Aspects of Narrative'. In the next chapters you will be shown ways to look in detail at this key concept in the study of literature. It is important to understand that this book helps you to work on skills rather than set books. Examples from literature will be used because they help to show a point. Sometimes they will be examples from the current set-text list, but not always – and anyway it might not be a text that you are doing.

💡 Storytelling

We are surrounded by storytelling, and on a basic level it forms an essential part of how we live. All cultures have storytelling as a vital part of human connection, and children, of course, are taught how to live within their culture by being told stories from a very young age.

Activity 1

On a piece of paper note down all the stories you have come into contact with in the last 24 hours. Then share one of them with your class as a whole.

🔍 *Commentary on Activity 1*

It is likely that you came up with plenty of examples of stories. The ones most people start with when doing this activity are the set pieces, coming from quite formal sources such as newspapers and magazines, and much more informal sources such as conversations about nights out with friends. You may, though, have spread your net wider. It can be argued that many of the visual texts that surround us wherever we go, advertising all sorts of products and services, tell us stories about our lives and our desires. And even the simplest of SMS texts from a friend might well be part of a bigger story.

■ Story/plot/narrative

In everyday use it does not really matter how we use the term 'story' because, after all, these stories flash past us at a rapid speed. We take from them as much as we want at any given time, and then pass on to the next.

When it comes to studying stories in a more academic way, however, it is useful to sort out some key terms and agree that they will be used in quite specific ways. As is always the case with such terminology, it is not important as such, but using it consistently helps to establish a common way of thinking and explaining – in this case about how literature works. Understanding the difference between the terms **story**, **plot** and **narrative** can help you to see where to focus your attention when reading the set texts for this unit.

💡 Key terms

Story: all the various events that are going to be shown.

Plot: the chain of causes and circumstances that connect the various events and place them into some sort of relationship with each other.

Narrative: involves how the events and causes are shown, and the various methods used to do this showing. Exploring aspects of narrative involves looking at what the writer has chosen to include or not include, and how this choice leads the reader to certain conclusions.

AQA Examiner's tip

Learn the distinction between the three key terms defined opposite and always use them accurately when writing about your set texts.

Representation

You will notice above that the word 'shown' has been used to describe the events in a story. This is because all stories are a form of **representation**. In terms of studying literature at AS-level there can be no more important concept to grasp than that of representation. Although when you read a text, or watch a film, or listen to a friend telling you about a night out you might for part of the time believe you are watching or hearing about something 'real', what you are actually doing is taking part in a constructed process. You are being shown something, being given a version. A film may seem incredibly realistic, but in the end it is still a film. Even a report of an event on a news broadcast, although originating in a real event, is a version of that event, shown by various narrative methods. The same goes for a friend telling you about a night out – even they are giving a version of events, almost certainly seen from their own perspective.

The logic of the paragraph above should be clear, then, for students of literature. Characters in literary texts, whether novels, plays or poems, are not real. Nor are the things that the characters do or say. They are representations of people living in a representational world. So, when studying literary texts, especially if you are looking at aspects of narrative, bear in mind the following simple rule:

It is the author who controls the characters and events in a story. Characters cannot do or say anything other than what the author makes them do.

For this reason, when asked to explore aspects of narrative in exams, it is vital to keep the authors, and their methods of working, at the heart of what you say.

Remember

Characters and events in stories are **representations** of reality, not real themselves, and are completely controlled by the author. Always bear the author's role in mind when you write about narrative in exams.

A true-life narrative

From what you have seen so far, it should be clear that while a story can be based upon real events, when it comes to telling the story we are dealing with a representation of what happened, rather than the actual event itself. However, this does not stop the producers of stories, whether in print or in film, from labelling their products as though they are 'real' or 'true'. After all, there is seemingly something more immediate and believable about a story that is trailed as having an intimate connection with the real world.

One genre that can be found easily on any magazine rack is the real-life story. Looking at an example from this genre is useful in setting out some of the aspects of narrative that you need to look at when studying literary texts.

Remember

A **genre** is a type of text (e.g. a crime novel, a narrative poem).

Activity 2

1. Look at the opening paragraphs of a story taken from *Woman's Own*. From your knowledge of other stories, and working with a partner if possible, try to list some of the ways in which the story is 'shown' to the reader. Remember: we are not dealing here with what happened, but with the methods the writer uses to represent events to the reader.

2. What do you think the overall message or moral of this story might be?

'He died a hero'

It was meant to be a relaxing family holiday by the seaside, but then tragedy struck …

Patricia Mangle took one last look at the paramedics trying to revive her husband. As a wife and mother, she had to make an agonising decision. She wanted to go with him in the helicopter, but her children needed her, too. As Steven was airlifted to hospital, she turned away, blinded by tears.

It would be the last time she saw her husband of 20 years alive.

Just an hour or so earlier, Patricia, a supermarket cashier, and Steven, 50, who worked for a refuse collection company, were happily relaxing outside the caravan in Skegness that they'd rented for four days. With them were their two youngest children, Mark, 16, and Laura, 12, with two of their friends, Josh, 16, and Laura-Beth, 13.

'It was teatime on 19 July, the hottest day of the year, and Steve and the kids were keen to get down to the beach,' says Patricia.

'I needed to stay and tidy up a bit, so they all went on ahead.

'From what Laura and Mark have told me since, Steve and the four children were splashing about in the water, when the sea suddenly changed and became choppy.

'Concerned for everyone's safety, Steve ordered the four youngsters out of the water, swimming with them towards the shore.

Then behind him, he suddenly heard screams for help. A young girl was caught in the waves.'

Eyewitnesses have told how Steven managed to swim against the tide, then reach the girl, aged 13, before pushing her to safety in shallower water. But the current was too strong for him.

'He was pulled under and didn't resurface. Two men on the beach raced to his aid and pulled him out of the sea, but by then it was too late,' says Patricia, her voice strained with emotion …

Woman's Own, 30 October 2006

Link

This article is discussed again in Unit 2, Chapter 9.

Commentary on Activity 2

Looking closely at aspects of narrative involves understanding that the same story can be told in a number of ways. In working out how an author has told the story, you then inevitably think about why the author might have done it this way, what effects the author has possibly been aiming for, and whether you as a reader find these effects interesting and convincing.

Each chapter in this unit will discuss one of the main aspects, or 'building blocks', of narrative that feature in this article. These are summarised below.

The building blocks of narrative

Scenes and places

This refers to where the action is set, and its significance beyond just being a place where something happens. So although this story is set in the seaside town of Skegness, there is wider significance to the scene. This involves the idea of the family holiday, of getting away from work – but also the hidden and sudden tragedy that can come out of any happy moment.

Time and sequence

The order in which events are shown is a key part of how narrative works. While **time** in the real world is represented by clocks and calendars which tick over at the same regular rate, time in stories is manipulated so that some points in time go slowly, others accelerate and others are missed out altogether. In this story we move very quickly to 'teatime on 19 July' before slowing right down as the tragedy unfolds.

Sequence meanwhile refers to the order in which events are told. Although at a very simple level all narratives involve a movement from a beginning to an end, they are rarely told in strict sequence. So here the first paragraph begins towards the end of the story, the third moves us back an hour. The reason for this should be obvious: if as readers we are to be interested in the story we need some action at the start.

Characters

Character in this sense refers not just to the people in the story but, much more importantly, to their character traits and how they are revealed: this is known as **characterisation**. It would be fair to say that here there are two main characters, Patricia Mangle and Steven Mangle. They are frequently referred to in terms of family relationships: 'husband', 'wife', 'mother', for example. Patricia is forced to make an 'agonising decision' based on the fact that she is both wife and mother. While Patricia tidies up, Steve is more active – they are cast in typical gendered roles. Steve is also a man with a sense of duty, who looks after all children, not just his own.

Meanwhile there is also a cast of more minor characters: their children who are named, and the young girl who is rescued who is not named.

Woman's Own is a magazine which has a certain presumed readership – women who have children. Not surprisingly in a magazine which constructs its readers as women in family relationships, this story, despite being 'tragic', is very positive about notions of family, duty and heroism.

Voices in the story

One way in which we get information in a story is through what we are 'told' by characters involved. There are various ways of showing this, which will be looked at in detail later, but here we hear directly from Patricia – 'It was teatime on 19 July …' – and more indirectly from her children: 'From what Mark and Laura have told me since'. Note too that although we are not given their precise words, what 'eyewitnesses' have reported is also given to us. These are not the actual words they would have spoken though – they are a tidied-up version of them, a representation of what they probably said.

Voices in stories can help to establish character traits, and so are part of **characterisation**, but they also enable authors to give information.

Point of view

In the section above one key voice in the text has not been mentioned: the voice of the narrator, standing outside the story. Although we are not told who wrote this story, it is told in the voice of a third person; it is a **third-person narrative**. One option available to the magazine was to tell the story entirely through the voice of Patricia. In this case it would have been a **first-person narrative**. The term **point of view** is used to help with the idea that a story is told from a certain standpoint or perspective. (You might notice here that the words used to describe narrative are often derived from visual metaphors.)

Key terms

Third-person narrative: a story told through the voice of a narrator who is not one of the characters in the story.

First-person narrative: a story told through the voice of one of the characters, using 'I'.

Key terms

Speaker: the person whose voice is heard in a poem, as opposed to the author.

Ideology: the attitudes, values and assumptions that the text contains, and which readers are expected to share – although they do not actually have to. Attitudes are to do with the approach taken to the subject matter; values are related to the beliefs expressed in the text; and assumptions are those things that are taken for granted and so do not need saying at all.

Just as the voices in the text are created voices, so are narrative voices. It is tempting, especially in poems, to confuse the voice that speaks a poem with the voice of the actual author. Avoid doing this at all times! You will find that questions in the examination sometimes refer to the **speaker** of the poem – this is a useful term which is well worth using.

Destination

So far you have looked at some of the ways in which stories can be told. But for this storytelling process to have any real purpose, you need to understand that the whole process is designed to make readers think, to make them respond to what has been said, to make them see the point or points. You have been taken on a journey in the story, and when you reach the end, you have reached a destination.

Although you have not been given the full story here, it is easy enough to work out what the destination, or morals, of the story could be:

- Tragedy is potentially everywhere.
- Love endures and alleviates at least some pain.
- Family ties are the strongest of all.

In working out that the story has moral messages, ideas that we are expected to believe in, we can see that the **ideology** of the story needs to be uncovered and explored. It is the assumptions made by the author that can often be the most interesting to find in texts: here for example we are expected to believe in the notion of the family, so this belief is never actually stated.

There are two final points to make here. As individual readers you may have seen some different points to the story from those given here. And although you may understand what you are meant to think, you may want to resist the most obvious message for various reasons. This means that in applying an analysis of narrative methods (AO2) you have come up with different interpretations (AO3) depending on the contexts in which you have read the story (AO4). In other words, you have made all the necessary connections that are involved in reading texts.

Link

The Assessment Objectives (AOs) 1–4 are explained in full in the Introduction to this book.

Making a building out of the blocks

Each of the next six chapters explores one of the aspects set out above, using prose and poetry as examples. It is important to remember, though, that all these aspects work together to form a complete narrative: separating them out at this stage can help you to understand how narrative works, but when it comes to exams you will be expected to draw on your knowledge of all the aspects, and decide which ones are most relevant in writing about your chosen text. To make sure that this is clear, each chapter concludes by looking at the same text, Robert Browning's poem *The Patriot*. At the end of the work on Unit 1, these aspects can be combined to look at the poem overall.

Summary

This chapter has introduced you to the key aspects of narrative, and to the fundamental point that when stories are told, they are representations of the world, not the world itself. Once you have grasped this key point, it is then possible to explore and analyse the ways in which stories are told, whether they are oral stories, popular journalism or literature.

AQA Examiner's tip

Try to develop a specialist vocabulary for English Literature which looks at large issues, rather than tiny (and sometimes irrelevant) details. It is no doubt true that using the correct terminology makes you seem well-informed and in the know. But equally important is the fact that using terminology accurately lets you write much more quickly and economically about your ideas and interpretations.

Scenes and places

Fictional stories, if they are to represent in some ways the real world, need to be set in significant places. These places can vary in size: they can be rooms, houses, gardens, streets, towns, regions, countries, worlds and even universes. They can be recognisable as places we already know, based on places we know but also clearly fictional, or completely invented 'new' worlds.

 These places though, all share something in common: they are **representations** of places, not actual places. At one end of the spectrum, a highly realistic description of an actual place that can be found on a map is still a version of the place in words, a depiction by an author of some aspects of the place but not others. At the other end of the spectrum, a completely invented place, that cannot possibly exist in our real world, will none the less have all sorts of features from our world that we can recognise. Between these two extremes, authors take bits of real places and alter them to suit their purposes.

Stories are condensed versions of reality, shaped to present actions and ideas that tell us something about the lives we lead. Stories need to be set in places if they are to persuade us of their connections with our lives, but at the same time these places can be more than just settings where events happen. Scenes and places frequently carry a significance that goes way beyond being where something merely happens. In their use of scenes and places, authors are taking advantage of the possibilities of creating meanings.

i Activity 1

From your own knowledge, and using research facilities such as the internet, histories of literature, etc. make a list of novels that have a place as a major part of their title. Does the name of this place carry connotations of meaning? You could then extend the search to include films and television programmes, especially soap operas, and again consider the possible significance of the places.

There is no commentary with this activity.

Place and significance

Thomas Hardy dated his poem *The Darkling Thrush* to signify that he was writing about the last day of the 19th century. In the poem he describes a natural place, and from this he goes on to make a more significant statement.

Activity 2

Read the poem at least twice – with this poem in particular it helps to hear it read aloud. Then consider the following questions:

1 What sort of place does Hardy describe and what details does he provide?

2 How does Hardy relate the setting of the poem to wider and more significant issues?

The Darkling Thrush

I leant upon a coppice gate
When Frost was spectre-gray,
And Winter's dregs made desolate
The weakening eye of day.
The tangled bine-stems scored the sky
Like strings of broken lyres,
And all mankind that haunted nigh
Had sought their household fires.

The land's sharp features seemed to be
The Century's corpse outleant,
His crypt the cloudy canopy,
The wind his death-lament.
The ancient pulse of germ and birth
Was shrunken hard and dry,
And every spirit upon earth
Seemed fervourless as I.

At once a voice arose among
The bleak twigs overhead
In a full-hearted evensong
Of joy illimited;
An aged thrush, frail, gaunt, and small,
In blast-beruffled plume,
Had chosen thus to fling his soul
Upon the growing gloom.

So little cause for carolings
Of such ecstatic sound
Was written on terrestrial things
Afar or nigh around,
That I could think there trembled through
His happy good-night air
Some blessed Hope, whereof he knew
And I was unaware.

Thomas Hardy, 31 December 1900

Commentary on Activity 2

Each of the verses in this poem has a distinct job, building up the layers of significance.

Verse 1: In this first verse Hardy chooses to describe a bleak, winter scene – after all, it is December. The frost looks ghost-like, the effect of the light is desolate, the twigs and branches are without leaves.

Verse 2: There are similar grim features in this verse, but this time they are compared to the laid-out body of the century that has just passed. By making a clear comparison between the 'land's sharp features' and 'the century's corpse', Hardy is clearly connecting the minor significance of where he is with the major significance of the passing century. Everything is 'shrunken hard and dry' and the speaker of the poem compares this natural description with his own mood – a frequent poetic device.

Verse 3: This verse provides a complete contrast. Although the thrush itself seems bedraggled and gaunt, it appears to sing 'of joy illimited'.

Verse 4: In this final verse Hardy weighs up the implications of the disparity between the scene around him, and by implication the hopes of a new century, and this beautiful and positive birdsong. In apparently plain and straightforward language, laced with religious ideas, he gives a subtly complex message about the future.

What we can see from this reading of *The Darkling Thrush* is that setting has been used in at least three ways:

- On a literal level it is the place where people and creatures live.
- On a more associative level, the setting has told us something about the characteristics and circumstances of the speaker of the poem.
- On a deeper level still the place stands not just for circumstances but for whole ways of seeing the world, of sets of beliefs and values. In this sense, therefore, the setting takes on a **symbolic** function.

As with all the examples you look at in this book while learning about aspects of narrative, your attention is being drawn to one aspect at a time. Inevitably, though, there are other aspects of narrative at work here too. If you return to this poem once you have read all the chapters on narrative, you will notice that it too has voices (including the thrush itself), thought, aspects of time, and so on, all contributing to its overall narrative structure and meanings.

A short walk or a whole life?

We have seen above that places can be used as locations for stories, but also as contributors to the wider significances of the stories being told. This section looks at a variant on the idea of the significance of place – the recurring **metaphor** that our life is a journey.

In their book *Metaphors We Live By* (1980), George Lakoff and Mark Johnson show how metaphors are not just used in literature, but also in our everyday speech and thinking. In some ways, reality itself is defined by the metaphors we commonly use to describe it; but because these metaphors are so common, we are often not even aware that we are speaking metaphorically.

One of the most ubiquitous of all metaphorical fields involves describing change and development in terms of a journey.

This same metaphor of the journey exists in many literary texts as well as films. So called 'road' novels and films are a distinct genre in themselves. Frequently the road and the journey serve as literal settings for action to take place, but as the journey progresses we are frequently aware that the main character (or characters) is learning from their experiences and becoming a new and altered person, usually wiser and more knowledgeable. As the journey develops, so does the individual.

In his much anthologised poem *The Road Not Taken*, the poet Robert Frost gives a variant on the road theme: he gives us a person standing at a crossroads, deciding which path to take. The idea of the crossroads is, of course, a common one in everyday life – we frequently refer to ourselves and others as being at a crossroads, when we are referring to potentially life-changing decisions.

AQA Examiner's tip

When answering an exam question, make sure you do exactly what is asked:

- In Section A you will be asked to look in detail at how the story is told in one of your set texts.
- In Section B the questions are much broader, asking you to write about an aspect of narrative across the other three texts you have studied.

These questions require different approaches.

Key terms

Symbolic: a symbol involves the reader making meanings and connections that are not directly stated (in contrast to **metaphor**, defined below).

Metaphor: metaphor involves the transfer of meaning, with one thing described as another. When one thing is described as being *like* another it is known as a **simile**.

Activity 3

Draw up a list of phrases that are commonly used to describe what happens in a lesson or lecture, and which refer metaphorically to a journey. Here are three to get you started:

- A lesson begins
- Pupils make progress
- Pupils get stuck.

Link

For a Commentary on Activity 3, see the end of this chapter (p17).

Did you know?

Lines and phrases from this poem are often quoted in order to suggest that unconventional people are the ones who succeed in life.

■ Activity 4

Read the poem below and see if you can find different possible meanings for the way Frost uses the 'two roads' in this poem.

The Road Not Taken

Two roads diverged in a yellow wood,
And sorry I could not travel both
And be one traveler, long I stood
And looked down one as far as I could
To where it bent in the undergrowth.

Then took the other, as just as fair,
And having perhaps the better claim,
Because it was grassy and wanted wear;
Though as for that the passing there
Had worn them really about the same.

And both that morning equally lay
In leaves no step had trodden black.
Oh, I kept the first for another day!
Yet knowing how way leads on to way,
I doubted if I should ever come back.

I shall be telling this with a sigh
Somewhere ages and ages hence:
Two roads diverged in a wood, and I –
I took the one less traveled by,
And that has made all the difference.

Robert Frost, 1920

Commentary on Activity 4

If you read this poem a number of times, its apparent simplicity becomes, if anything, ever more complex. Clearly one way to read the poem is to stick with the idea that it is about having the nerve to make the unconventional life choice, but the more you read the poem, the more of a problem that simple reading can become.

Where poems are so clearly structured in their verse patterns, it can often help to take one verse at a time and see how the argument moves forward. Here we have four verses of five lines each.

Verse 1: Here the dilemma is set up: there are two paths, and although the speaker (who we will assume is male) would like to travel down both, he knows that he can only choose one. None the less he takes his time and tries to peer ahead down one route (that is, into the future) to see if it is worth taking.

Verse 2: Somewhat surprisingly, he chooses the one he has not considered much. This one is the one that is less worn – but actually it is a close-run thing between the two. The choices are not that different.

Verse 3: Again he tells us that there is not much to choose between the two paths, and that on that morning they were in fact identical! He decides to keep one for another day (so it is not a major decision) while at the same time knowing that he will probably never come back to take the other path.

Verse 4: We now come to the final verse, and the lines we have already seen quoted out of context. They are put in a different context, though, by the two lines that precede them. The chronology of the poem, its time sequence, makes reference to both the present, the future and, in the last lines, a sort of future/past. Out of context, of course the final three lines look sure and definitive, but in context there is much more ambiguity. The fact that the speaker knows he will be 'telling this with a sigh' makes the choice seem far less obviously 'right'. A sigh seems to suggest possible regret, for example.

Not surprisingly this poem has received a huge amount of critical survey. Whatever the reading of the poem, most critics see the crossroads as highly symbolic. Just to add to the ambiguity, though, Frost himself denied that the poem was meant to have huge significance. He claimed the poem was about his friend and fellow poet Edward Thomas, who was horribly indecisive and could not even make up his mind which path to take without making a fuss about it!

Link

For more on time and chronology see Chapter 3.

Places in prose fiction

Places have a significant role in prose fiction. In a poem, with its concise narrative, specifics of a place can be given without all the detail of precise location. In the poem above, we do not know where the paths actually are, in which village. Indeed, the absence of any precise location helps us to think that the paths could be anywhere, which makes the significance more widely applicable.

In prose fiction, though, there is a greater expectation that places will be filled out in detail. There is more room in novels and stories, and readers have the expectation that places will be described more fully. In novels and stories people's lives are examined in detail, and although these lives are fictional, in most cases we expect them to be 'realistic', to represent a world we recognise. (There are, of course, always exceptions to rules about literature: science fiction and fantasy, for example, tend to describe weird and exotic places, even if in some ways such genres still comment on the actual world as we know it.)

Not surprisingly, then, there is a tradition in English literature of novelists who centre their work on one particular place or area. Dickens frequently writes about London, representing real places with their actual names. Hardy does something slightly different: although his novels are largely set in the area around Dorset, he uses the older name of Wessex for the area, and changes the names of towns, with Dorchester becoming Casterbridge, for example.

When authors set a novel in a known geographical area, they also have the opportunity to represent people who live in that area by giving a version of their **dialect**. In this case the dialect can refer to grammar, vocabulary and pronunciation.

At the start of the novel *Fingersmith* by Sarah Waters, set in London in 1862, the narrator Susan describes how Flora and she went pickpocketing and brought back some stolen perfume to the woman who looks after them, Mrs Sucksby.

AQA Examiner's tip

You are encouraged at AS to consider different possible interpretations of the same piece of text. Meanings are not fixed, and you are not expected to say one interpretation is 'right'. It is perfectly acceptable, though, to give a personal preference.

Key terms

Dialect: regional and sometimes social variations in language.

'What you get? A couple of wipers was it? A couple of wipers, and a lady's purse?'

Flora pulled the strand of hair to her mouth and bit it. 'A purse,' she said, after a second. 'And a bottle of scent.'…

Mrs Sucksby sniffed.

'Pretty poor poke,' she said, 'ain't it?'

Flora tossed her head. 'I should have had more,' she said, with a look at me, 'if she hadn't started up with the sterics.'

Mrs Sucksby leaned and hit her again.

'If I had known what you was about,' she said, 'you shouldn't have none of it at all. Let me tell you now, you want an infant for prigging with, you take one of my other babies.'

Sarah Waters, Fingersmith, 2003, pp4–5

Here Sarah Waters uses occasional items of vocabulary and grammar to represent local speech and also social class. So in vocabulary there is 'poke' for 'smell', 'sterics' for 'hysterics', 'prigging' for 'stealing'. And in grammar there is 'ain't it' for 'isn't it', 'you was' for 'you were' and the double negative 'shouldn't have none'. There is no attempt as such though to represent the accent, the distinctive local sounds – the word 'bottle' for example is written in standard form, and it is left to the reader to imagine how this might sound.

This literary representation of talk can be taken further by adding some sense of sound. This involves using what is known as **eye-dialect**.

In Thomas Hardy's *Tess of the D'Urbervilles*, a local woman meets a stranger to the area:

'Well, I suppose you'll want a dish o' tay, or victuals of some sort hey?'

Emily Bronte's use of the servant Joseph in *Wuthering Heights* takes this method to a greater extreme:

'If Aw wur yah, maister, Aw'd just slam t'boards I' their faces, all on em'.

The gap

Although locations in fiction are necessary arenas for people and their actions to take place in, these locations can also carry greater significance, much as we saw in the poems earlier. The places are not only venues where things happen; they throw extra light and significance on events, people and relationships.

In his story *Abyss*, the American writer Richard Ford writes about Howard and Frances, two estate agents who are having an affair while attending a conference. Instead of attending the conference, they decide to bunk off and instead visit the Grand Canyon in Arizona. The Grand Canyon is described as follows on its national park website:

The Grand Canyon is more than a great chasm carved over millennia through the rocks of the Colorado Plateau. It is more than an awe-inspiring view. It is more than a pleasuring ground for those that explore the roads, hike the trails, or float the currents of the turbulent Colorado River.

This canyon is a gift that transcends what we experience. Its beauty and size humbles us. Its timelessness provokes a comparison to our short existence. In its vast spaces we may find solace from our hectic lives.

Link

For more on the importance of how characters speak in a story, see Chapter 4.

Key terms

Eye-dialect: the representation of the vocabulary, grammar and sound of dialect in a way the reader can understand, in contrast to the phonetic representation (with special symbols) that a linguist would use.

Did you know?

The Grand Canyon, in the US state of Arizona, is a vast and colourful gorge cut by the Colorado River over a period of about 6 million years. It is 277 miles (446 km) long, between 4 and 18 miles (6.4 to 24 km) wide, and more than a mile (1.6 km) deep.

Fig. 1 *The Grand Canyon*

Activity 5

Read again the tourist hype above, which gives the 'official' version of how tourists should perceive the Grand Canyon, and study the photo. Then consider the following questions:

1 Given that Ford could have chosen any location in which to set his story, what might happen in the plot to make his choice of the Grand Canyon especially significant?

2 What effects might the 'awe-inspiring' view of the canyon have on the two characters? How might they respond to the almost religious experience that the tourist hype suggests?

Activity 6

Now read the extract from Richard Ford's story *Abyss*. At this point in the story Frances and Howard actually reach the Grand Canyon. The story is told in the third person, but here it is very much told from the point of view of Howard. Answer the following questions:

1 In what ways do Howard and Frances react differently to their first experience of the Grand Canyon?

2 In the light of what you have discussed already about the significance of place, what use does Ford make of the Grand Canyon in this extract?

Link

For a Commentary on Activity 5, see the end of this chapter (p17).

Link

For more on point of view see Chapter 6.

Link

For a Commentary on Activity 6, see the end of this chapter (p17).

And then, all at once, just very suddenly, he was there; at the Grand Canyon, beside Frances who had her camera: up to her face. And there was no way really not to be surprised by it – the whole Grand Canyon just all right there at once, opened out and down and wide in front of you, enormous and bottomless, with a great invisible silence inhabiting it and a column of cool air pushing up out of it like a giant well. It was a shock.

'I don't want you to say one single thing,' Frances said. She wasn't looking through her camera now, but had begun to stare right into the canyon itself, like she was inhaling it. Sunlight was on her face. She seemed blissed.

He did, however, expect to say *something*. It was just natural to want to put some words of your own to the whole thing. Except he instantly had the feeling, standing beside Frances, that he was already doing something wrong, had somehow approached this wrong, or was standing wrong, even looking at the goddamned canyon wrong. And there was something about how you couldn't see it at all, and then you completely did see it, something that seemed to suggest you could actually miss it. Miss the whole Grand Canyon!

Of course, the right way would be to look at it all at once, taking in the full effect, just the way Frances seemed to be doing. Except it was much too big to get everything into focus. Too big and too complicated. He felt like he wanted to turn around, go back to the car and come up again. Get re-prepared.

Though it was exactly, he thought, staring mutely out at the flat brown plateau and the sheer drop straight off the other side – how far away, you couldn't tell, since perspective was screwed up – it was exactly what he'd expected from the pictures in high school. It was a tourist attraction. A thing to see. It was plenty big. But twenty jillion people had already seen it, so that it felt sort of useless. A negative. Nothing like the ocean, which *had* a use. Nobody *needed* the Grand Canyon for anything. At its most important, he guessed, it would be a terrific impediment to someone wanting to get to the other side. Which would not be a good comment to make to Frances, who was probably having a religious experience. She'd blow her top on that. The best comment, he thought, should be that it was really quiet. He'd never experienced anything this quiet. And it was nothing like an airport. Though flying in that little plane was probably the best way to see it.

Richard Ford, Abyss, 1996, pp270–1

The Patriot

As mentioned in Chapter 1, each of the chapters that looks at a different aspect of narrative concludes by looking at the same text, *The Patriot* by Robert Browning.

Activity 7

Read the poem and answer the following questions:

1. This poem has a setting. What details are you given about that setting?
2. Can you say precisely where that place is?

Extension tasks

1. Rewrite the extract taken from the short story *Abyss*, this time describing the Grand Canyon from the point of view of Frances. How does your version differ from the original?
2. Consider the novels that you are studying, and discuss the following issues:
   - What are the major locations where the novels are set?
   - How much space, roughly, do the authors give to describing places?
   - Do any of the places seem to be especially significant – if so, how?
   - Is speech used to represent the way local people might talk?
3. Now consider the poetry text or texts that you are studying and discuss the following:
   - Are scenes and places of any particular significance? If so, in what ways?
   - How have the authors signalled this significance to the reader?

Commentaries

Commentary on Activity 3

Among the other possibilities are:

- Going round in circles
- Moving ahead of the rest
- Finishing early
- Being lost
- Following an argument
- Straying from an argument
- Covering a lot of ground
- Going back over the same material
- Getting off the point
- Well on your way to making good progress
- Lagging behind the others
- Going off in the wrong direction.

Commentary on Activity 5

1   The title of the story gives a clue – an abyss is a huge hole, a gap, which is exactly what the Grand Canyon is. This idea of a gap in nature can easily be transferred to a gap in the relationship between the two characters.

2   The awe with which one is expected to view the canyon could go in a number of ways: the two characters could find perfect harmony, or far from bringing them together, the experience could drive them apart. Again, the title of the story gives a clue as to which is likely to be the case. If one or both of the characters does not respond to the almost religious experience that the tourist hype suggests, the location could be used to highlight something **not** happening, making a sort of contrast.

Commentary on Activity 6

1   Howard arrives at the canyon after Frances. She is clearly overwhelmed by the experience, or so Howard thinks. She tells him, 'I don't want you to say a single thing', and to Howard she 'seemed blissed'. Notice that although they do not say anything, Howard did expect to 'say something'. He seems to want to share the experience; she wants to experience it alone.

For Howard, therefore, the experience is unsettling, and in various ways unsatisfactory. Annoyed by being shut out by Frances, he is as bothered by her as he is by the canyon. He considers it possible to miss the whole thing, while on the other hand it is impossible to get it all into focus. Because so many others have seen it, he finds it 'sort of useless'. All he can think of is that it stops you getting to the other side, whereas Frances seems to be finding it 'a religious experience'.

In other parts of the story Ford switches his perspective to Frances – we get a sense here that were she to be telling the story it would be very different.

2   What should be clear is that Ford has used the Grand Canyon as a vehicle to show the two lovers drifting apart, that what lies ahead of them, in terms of their relationship, is an abyss, a chasm. Ford needs to set the story of this failing relationship somewhere, because stories need to be placed. But in choosing this venue, he has given himself the opportunity to make the place stand for more than just a location. The alert reader recognises the connections between where a story is set and what the story is saying.

Commentary on Activity 7

1 There are a few details about the setting. It seems to be a walled town or even a city, given that we are told there are 'church-spires' in the plural. The reference to 'house-roofs' might imply a place of some grandeur.

2 Although the brief references to setting may remind you of a certain type of city – York maybe – in fact there is nothing very precise about the location. Not even the country is specified.

Summary

This chapter has explored the significance of places in stories. Even if the places actually exist, in the representational world of stories certain details will have been selected to help make a point. Looking at the significance of places is therefore one way to explore narrative technique.

3 Time and sequence

Aims of the chapter:

- Describes the importance in stories of time and sequence.

- Explains that because stories are representational, time in stories needs to be compressed.

- Shows how time in stories can be rearranged, repeated, speeded up and slowed down.

- Demonstrates that in fictional worlds things happen only when the writer chooses.

Remember

AO2 and AO4 are two of the four Assessment Objectives discussed in the Introduction to this book.

Key terms

Chronological order: the sequence of events as they happen, in a timeline that goes from A, the start of events, to say E, the end.

Remember

A **genre** is a type of text, such as a crime novel or a narrative poem, so a sub-genre is a particular type of text within that genre.

All stories, however fantastic their genre, need to have aspects of time. The word 'aspects' is in the plural because even in this broad sense time can work in at least two ways:

1 The time covered by the events within the story.
2 The broader time which surrounds the story, the time in which the story is set.

For example, if a contemporary novelist writes a love story, the time covered by events might be from the time the couple meet to the time they marry (or divorce?). But if the author wants to write a love story set in Victorian times, then other aspects of time are involved – if the story is to appear believable then the author will have to incorporate aspects of Victorian life and attitudes (which probably would not lead to divorce!). In a general sense, then (general because as always these aspects of narrative overlap), how the author manages time *within* the story is covered by AO2, which looks at aspects of form, structure and language, in this case with a special focus on structure. Meanwhile, how the author manages time which *surrounds* the story is covered by AO4, which looks at contexts.

So if the story is to involve a sequence of events, how the sequence is presented to the reader be of considerable importance.

Chronology

If we were all to write our stories, whether 'real' or 'imagined', in strict **chronological order**, two main issues would arise:

1 Telling a story in strict chronological order can be very dull – one of the first lessons children have to learn when writing stories is not to start at the beginning (and maybe not even end at the end).
2 Is it actually possible with a complex story to say definitively that it has a beginning and an end anyway? In a complex world, such hard-and-fast distinctions are not always possible – and writers, of course, are aware of this.

Imagine, as an example, that you are going to write a piece of crime fiction, which will have a murder as its main 'crime'. Immediately you are faced with all sorts of narrative questions, but for the moment concentrate on aspects of sequence. Questions you will have to consider include:

- Does the story start with the body being discovered?
- Does the story start with the murder itself?
- Does the story start with the planning of the murder?
- Does the story start with the detective being called to the case?

If you think this through, it should be clear to you that how you answer this question potentially points to the type, or **sub-genre**, of crime fiction you are going to write. If you start with the discovery of the body, you might be writing a forensic novel where the perpetrator is uncovered through evidence; if you start with the planning of the murder, then the murderer will be known to the reader but not to the detective.

And when you have sorted this out, you have to ask yourself: What comes next?

Activity 1

Look at the three different comic-strip chains below, showing how the same murder story can be told in different sequences. Then write an outline for a crime story of your own, and work out different chronological sequences for the key events. How would your story's genre change depending on the sequences you choose? If you are working in a class setting you can also compare stories with a partner.

There is no commentary with this activity.

If we take as an example a typical plot line from a detective story, its chronological sequence might be something like this:

1 A murder is planned for a certain motive.
2 A body is found which yields evidence.
3 The detective pursues a number of clues and identifies the killer.
4 A violent shoot-out leads to the death of the villain.
5 This leads to another revenge killing.

It is easy to conceive, however, other ways of presenting this sequence – for example it could go 4, 1, 2, 3, 5 or 2, 1, 3, 4, 5. In each case something different would be foregrounded by the chronology. Chronology, then, is one way in which the writer of a narrative can influence the way a reader responds to it. This can lead to a focus on suspense, where the action and its results are foregrounded, or on character, where feelings are foregrounded, or sometimes both.

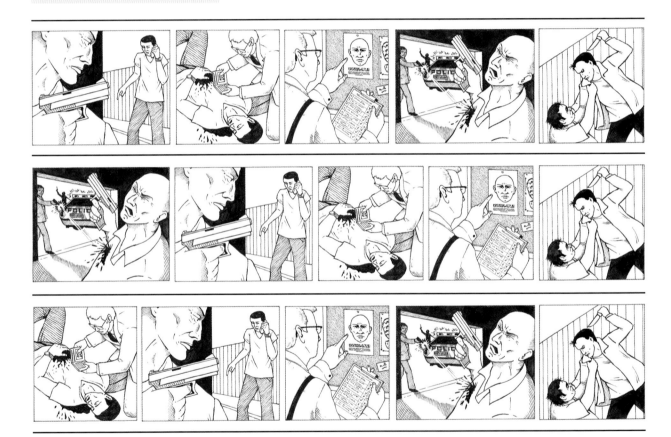

Fig. 1

Aspects of time in poetry and novels

Your work for this unit on Aspects of Narrative includes looking at both novels and poems. Poems by definition tend to be briefer exercises in narrative than novels. Whereas in a novel we expect some detailed **establishment**, in terms of place, time, people, and so on in poems we tend to be straight in and out of the story with much less detail. Indeed the effects of the poem are often emphasised by what is not given, by what can be called meaningful **absence**.

We will begin by looking at examples of time and sequence in poems.

AQA Examiner's tip

It is always worth thinking about the differences in the ways in which novels and poems can tell stories.

Time and sequence in poetry

O What Is That Sound?

O what is that sound which so thrills the ear
Down in the valley drumming, drumming?
Only the scarlet soldiers, dear,
The soldiers coming.

O what is that light I see flashing so clear
Over the distance brightly, brightly?
Only the sun on their weapons, dear,
As they step lightly.

O what are they doing with all that gear
What are they doing this morning, this morning?
Only the usual manoeuvres, dear,
Or perhaps a warning.

O why have they left the road down there
Why are they suddenly wheeling, wheeling?
Perhaps a change in the orders, dear,
Why are you kneeling?

O haven't they stopped for the doctor's care
Haven't they reined their horses, their horses?
Why, they are none of them wounded, dear,
None of these forces.

O is it the parson they want with white hair;
Is it the parson, is it, is it?
No, they are passing his gateway, dear,
Without a visit.

O it must be the farmer who lives so near
It must be the farmer so cunning, so cunning?
They have passed the farm already, dear,
And now they are running.

O where are you going? stay with me here!
Were the vows you swore me deceiving, deceiving?
No, I promised to love you, dear,
But I must be leaving.

O it's broken the lock and splintered the door,
O it's the gate where they're turning, turning
Their feet are heavy on the floor
And their eyes are burning.

W.H. Auden, 1934

Activity 2

In W.H. Auden's ballad-type poem *O What Is That Sound?* two voices take it in turns to speak. Here they have been distinguished by different typefaces, although that is not always the way the poem is presented. Read the poem at least twice, preferably aloud, and then answer the following questions:

1 When is this poem set in terms of its 'surrounding' time?

2 Is the action of the poem chronological?

3 Does the action of the poem have a clear beginning and end?

4 How do your answers to the questions above contribute to your understanding of the poem's overall meanings and effects?

Commentary on Activity 2

1 We are told that the poem was written in 1934, and that perhaps alerts us to the fact that it was written at a time of growing dictatorships and fascism in Europe. Yet at the same time the poem does not seem to be set in 1934: the soldiers drumming, the soldiers' uniforms, the suggestion that they might be carrying swords all suggest an earlier, less mechanised time. So to this extent the poem has no specific time reference. It also has no specific reference to place.

2 The action of the poem is indeed chronological, narrated from the watching perspective of the two speakers.

3 There is no beginning to the story: who are these people, where are they staying, why are they there? There is also no ending. Although the soldiers have arrived and broken down the door, we do not know if one of the lovers gets away or not and what happens to the other one.

4 Because there is so much absence of detail here, the poem opens up many possible meanings. Is it about oppression, with its insistent patterns of sound drumming out a warning about the individual's plight in the face of military might? Is it a spy story, with the spy getting away and leaving his lover to face the music? Is it a love story? The strength of the poem is that it sets up possibilities and ambiguities that make the reader work hard and return to the poem again and again. While novels can often also have their absences and ambiguities, it is fair to say that they tend to operate with less intensity than here.

Time and sequence in the modern novel

Unit 1 of your AS exam involves reading at least one modern novel – modern in that they were written from 1990 to the present day (another way in which literature can be viewed according to time!). However, just because a novel is written post-1990, that does not mean that it has to be set in that period of time. The novel *Birdsong* by Sebastian Faulks begins with a page saying:

PART ONE
France 1910

Here the author establishes three things with a minimum of fuss: that the novel is set in France, that the time is 1910 (even though the novel was published in 1993) and that time is unlikely to remain at that point, the implication being that part two will move to another year.

Andrea Levy in *Small Island* takes a less straightforward approach to time – remember, there is nothing that says a story has to be told chronologically. The first chapter of *Small Island* is called 'Prologue'. This is followed by a chapter entitled '1948'. Two chapters after this comes a chapter labelled 'Before'. So within 30 or so pages we have the following headings:

Prologue
1948
Before

Each one potentially deal with a different point of time, but with the implication that events are none the less connected.

> At eight o'clock in the evening, the Baltimore airport was nearly deserted. The wide gray corridors were empty, and the newsstands were dark, and the coffee shops were closed. Most of the gates had admitted their last flights. Their signboards were blank and their rows of vinyl chairs unoccupied and ghostly.
>
> But you could hear a distant hum, a murmur of anticipation, at the far end of Pier D. You could see an overexcited child spinning herself into dizziness in the center of the corridor, and then a grownup popping forth to scoop her up and carry her, giggling and squirming, back into the waiting area. And a latecomer, a woman in a yellow dress, was rushing toward the gate with an armful of long-stemmed roses.

Activity 3

Anne Tyler's novel *Digging to America* is about the assimilation of Korean orphans into American culture. As the novel begins, various family members are awaiting the arrival of the children whom they are going to adopt, but whom they have never seen before. What do you notice about the treatment of time as the novel begins?

Step around the bend, then, and you'd come upon what looked like a gigantic baby shower. The entire waiting area for the flight from San Francisco was packed with people bearing pink- and blue-wrapped gifts, or hanging on to flotillas of silvery balloons printed with IT'S A GIRL! and trailing spirals of pink ribbon. A man gripped the wicker handle of a wheeled and skirted bassinet as if he planned to roll it onto the plane, and a woman stood ready with a stroller so chrome-trimmed and bristling with levers that it seemed capable of entering the Indy 500. At least half a dozen people held video cameras, and many more had regular cameras slung around their necks. A woman spoke into a tape recorder in an urgent, secretive way. The man next to her clasped an infant's velour-upholstered car-seat close to his chest.

MOM, the button on the woman's shoulder read – one of those laminated buttons such as you might see in an election year. And the man's read DAD. A nice-looking couple, not as young as you might expect – the woman in wide black pants and an arty black-and-white top of a geometric design, her short hair streaked with gray; the man a big, beaming jovial type with a stubbly blond buzz cut, his bald knees poking bashfully from voluminous khaki Bermudas.

And not only were there MOM and DAD; there were GRANDMA and GRANDPA, twice over – two complete sets. One grandma was a rumpled, comfortable woman in a denim sundress and bandanna-print baseball cap; the other was thin and gilded and expertly made up, wearing an ecru linen pantsuit and dyed-to-match pumps. The grandpas were dyed to match as well – the rumpled woman's husband equally rumpled, his iron-gray curls overdue for a cutting, while the gilded woman's husband wore linen trousers and some sort of gauzy tropical shirt, and part of his bright yellow hair was possibly not his own.

Anne Tyler, Digging to America, *pp4–5*

Commentary on Activity 3

The novel begins with a very exact time reference and at the same time a vague one. Although we know it is 'eight o'clock in the evening' we do not know what day or year it is. The significance of the point in time is that the airport is just about closed, the traffic of the day is gone – except for one flight. Immediately there is an air of expectation.

And as the narrative 'walks' us through the airport towards what was at first a 'distant hum', time moves remarkably slowly, almost as though we are in real time. There is enough time for lots of detail to be observed. What Ann Tyler is doing is building up the expectation, making the narrator/reader wait as long as the would-be parents.

A different author, writing a different novel, might have started with the explosive moment of the children arriving, but this is not Anne Tyler's method.

🔍 Time frames

Timescales can be deliberately manipulated by writers to help them create subtle effects and meanings. One way of doing this is to create what is often called a time frame, putting one story inside another. This 'frame' appears at the beginning of the story, and sometimes – but not always – at the end, and there can even be reminders of the different timescales elsewhere in the story.

Read the opening lines of Tennyson's poem *Godiva* and answer the following questions:

1. What timescales does Tennyson use in the poem, and how does he indicate these to the reader?

2. What meanings does Tennyson make through this use of a time frame?

■ **Did you know?**

In the legend of Lady Godiva her husband said he would grant her request to cut taxes if she would ride naked through the streets of Coventry. She did this clothed only in her long hair, while the townspeople stayed inside. Her husband kept his word.

■ Key terms

Archaic: belonging to a much earlier period; archaic vocabulary is 'old' words deliberately used to suggest an earlier time.

The gaps between the timescales can vary. In her novel *Frankenstein*, Mary Shelley's timescales are quite close together. In his poem *Godiva*, Tennyson separates events from over one thousand years. The legend of Godiva centres on the town of Coventry, where Lady Godiva acted against her husband in defence of the poor.

Godiva

I waited for the train at Coventry;
I hung with grooms and porters on the bridge,
To watch the three tall spires; and there I shaped
The city's ancient legend into this:

Not only we, the latest seed of Time,
New men, that in the flying of a wheel
Cry down the past, not only we, that prate
Of rights and wrongs, have loved the people well,
And loathed to see them overtax'd; but she
Did more, and underwent, and overcame,
The woman of a thousand summers back,
Godiva, wife to that grim Earl, who ruled
In Coventry: for when he laid a tax
Upon his town, and all the mothers brought
Their children, clamoring, 'If we pay, we starve!'
She sought her lord, and found him, where he strode
About the hall, among his dogs, alone,
His beard a foot before him and his hair
A yard behind. She told him of their tears,
And pray'd him, 'If they pay this tax, they starve.'
Whereat he stared, replying, half-amazed,
'You would not let your little finger ache
For such as these?' – 'But I would die,' said she.

Alfred Tennyson, 1842

Commentary on Activity 4

1. Writing in the first person, the narrator compares himself on a bridge at Coventry station with events in the town 'a thousand summers back'. By referring to the station he is deliberately using something very modern (at least to Victorians) and he reinforces this by references to 'new men' and 'the flying of a wheel'.

   Once he begins to tell the story of Godiva, though, other aspects of time can be noticed. He begins the story with Godiva telling her husband of the people's poverty and the verb tense 'would' suggests something possibly to happen in the future.

2. Various effects can be seen in this use of a time frame. The story is given a context, which allows Tennyson to use rather **archaic** vocabulary to simulate ancient times. The most significant meaning, though, is not about the past, as such, but about Tennyson's view of the present. He is saying here that his own age may think itself sophisticated, as exemplified by train travel, but the legend of Godiva gives a purer moral picture. While modern men 'prate/Of rights and wrongs', Godiva 'did more, and underwent and overcame'. People in those times were 'overtax'd' not just financially but by the burdens of life itself.

Time and cause

A tendency in modern fiction, or at least in the sub-genre called 'literary fiction', has been to show that meaning is relative, that even apparently the most simple of incidents has a string of causes and motives that cannot easily be untangled. One way of highlighting this position is to consider aspects of time – although, as has been suggested many times already, there are other aspects of narrative involved too.

Activity 5

Below is the opening of Ian McEwan's novel *Enduring Love*. It is narrated by Joe Rose, a middle-aged man who is a science journalist. He is having a picnic with his girlfriend Clarissa, when he sees a child in a balloon. Read the extract carefully, and make notes in response to the following questions:

1. What references to time can you find here, and what might they tell you about the novel's ideas?

2. What is significant, do you think, about the last sentence in this extract?

The beginning is simple to mark. We were in sunlight under a turkey oak, partly protected from a strong, gusty wind. I was kneeling on the grass with a corkscrew in my hand, and Clarissa was passing me the bottle – a 1987 Daumas Gassac. This was the moment, this was the pinprick on the time map: I was stretching out my hand, and as the cool neck and the black foil touched my palm, we heard a man's shout. We turned to look across the field and saw the danger. Next thing, I was running towards it. The transformation was absolute: I don't recall dropping the corkscrew, or getting to my feet, or making a decision, or hearing the caution Clarissa called after me. What idiocy, to be racing into this story and its labyrinths, sprinting away from our happiness among the fresh spring grasses by the oak. There was the shout again, and a child's cry, enfeebled by the wind that roared in the tall trees along the hedgerows. I ran faster. And there, suddenly, from different points around the field, four other men were converging on the scene, running like me.

I see us from three hundred feet up, through the eyes of the buzzard we had watched earlier, soaring, circling and dipping in the tumult of currents: five men running silently towards the centre of a hundred-acre field. I approached from the south-east, with the wind at my back. About two hundred yards to my left two men ran side by side. They were farm labourers who had been repairing the fence along the field's southern edge where it skirts the road. The same distance beyond them was the motorist, John Logan, whose car was banked on the grass verge with its door, or doors, wide open. Knowing what I know now, it's odd to evoke the figure of Jed Parry directly ahead of me, emerging from a line of beeches on the far side of the field a quarter of a mile away, running into the wind. To the buzzard Parry and I were tiny forms, our white shirts brilliant against the green, rushing towards each other like lovers, innocent of the grief this entanglement would bring. The encounter that would unhinge us was minutes away, its enormity disguised from us not only by the barrier of time but by the colossus in the centre of the field that drew us in with the power of a terrible ratio that set fabulous magnitude against the puny human distress at its base.

What was Clarissa doing? She said she walked quickly towards the centre of the field. I don't know how she resisted the urge to run. By the time it happened – the event I am about to describe, the fall – she had almost caught us up and was well placed as an observer, unencumbered by participation, by the ropes and the shouting, and by our fatal lack of co-operation. What I describe is shaped by what Clarissa saw too, by what we told each other in the time of obsessive re-examination that followed: the aftermath, an appropriate term for what happened in a field waiting for its early summer mowing. The aftermath, the second crop, the growth promoted by that first cut in May.

I'm holding back, delaying the information. I'm lingering in the prior moment because it was a time when other outcomes were still possible; the convergence of six figures in a flat green space has a comforting geometry from the buzzard's perspective, the knowable, limited plane of the snooker table. The initial conditions, the force and the direction of the force, define all the consequent pathways, all the angles of collision and return, and the glow of the overhead light bathes the field, the baize and all its moving bodies, in reassuring clarity. I think that while we were still converging, before we made contact, we were in a state of mathematical grace. I linger on our dispositions, the relative distances and the compass point – because as far as these occurrences were concerned, this was the last time I understood anything clearly at all.

What were we running towards? I don't think any of us would ever know fully. But superficially the answer was, a balloon. Not the nominal space that encloses a cartoon character's speech or thought, or, by analogy, the kind that's driven by mere hot air. It was an enormous balloon filled with helium, that elemental gas forged from hydrogen in the nuclear furnace of the stars, first step along the way in the generation of multiplicity and variety of matter in the universe, including our selves and all our thoughts.

We were running towards a catastrophe, which itself was a kind of furnace in whose heat identities and fates would buckle into new shapes. At the base of the balloon was a basket in which there was a boy, and by the basket, clinging to a rope, was a man in need of help.

Even without the balloon the day would have been marked for memory, though in the most pleasurable of ways, for this was a reunion after a separation of six weeks, the longest Clarissa and I had spent apart in our seven years.

Ian McEwan, Enduring Love, *pp1–3*

Link: extract 12

To complete Activity 6 you will need to use *The Patriot* which is printed in the Extracts section at the back of this book, extract 12.

The Patriot

We return to *The Patriot*, a poem by Robert Browning, written in the mid 19th century. The poem is narrated by a man about to be hanged.

Activity 6

1. Is it possible to say when this poem is set in terms of historical time?
2. What meanings can you find in the subtitle of the poem, 'An Old Story'?
3. What specific references to time are made in the poem?
4. How does understanding the poem's use of time and sequence open up possible meanings in the poem?

Extension tasks

1 Consider the novels that you are studying, and for each novel discuss the following issues:

▢ What timescale is covered by the novel?

▢ At what point in the timescale does the novel open in the first chapter?

▢ Map out an outline of the sequence of events in the novel. To what extent are they chronological?

▢ At what point in time does the novel end? Would you say this is the 'end' of the story and everything is complete?

▢ How significant overall is time to the way the story is told and to what its meanings are?

2 Consider the poetry texts that you are studying, and for each discuss the following issues:

▢ To what extent do the poems show aspects of time?

▢ What is the significance of time in the poem or poems?

▢ Does the poet use aspects of time to reflect on aspects of human existence?

▢ Is there any ambiguity about the time in which the poems are set? If so, what is the effect of this?

▉ Commentaries

Commentary on Activity 5

1 The first sentence is 'spoken' by Joe, but clearly Ian McEwan is immediately making a point here. Saying that 'The beginning is simple to mark' sounds very confident and assured, but by the end of this extract it is clear that the 'beginning' is not simple, and perhaps never can be. Causes of events, however strange and serious, are more complex than this. There is never really a 'pinprick' of time that is 'the moment'.

There are plenty of chronological time references as he races across the field, such as 'next thing' and 'suddenly', but then the action stops and we are brought forward in time to 'knowing what I know now'. But even that certainty is made more doubtful by references to 'an obsessive re-examination' in the 'aftermath' of what happened.

Meanwhile, partially hidden in the unfolding drama of the balloon is an event of much more significance as far as Joe is concerned: his encounter with Jed Parry whose significance, when it happened, was blocked by 'the barrier of time'. And as Joe ponders on this, time almost stops altogether.

2 The gap between the end of the first section and the start of the second is a sort of pause, and then as Joe continues he begins to chip away at what he claimed at the start. The story whose beginning was so easy to mark has already now gone back 'six weeks' and then 'seven years'.

Commentary on Activity 6

1 In terms of actual historical time there are few clues. The occasional reference, such as to 'Shambles' Gate' and the occasional **archaism**, such as 'trow', suggest quite a distant past, but in contextual terms there is no specific period of time.

2 The subtitle, which could suggest that the story is set in the distant past, is subtly ambiguous. Is this an old story because it is historical, or is it an old story because it is one told many times, with as much reference to now as to any other time?

3 There is a clear and precise timescale to the poem. The voice narrating the poem compares his public reception a year ago with his reception now. He is on his way to the scaffold, near the Shambles (where butchers traded), where a vast and aggressive crowd waits. It was at this point where a year ago he was feted with flowers. The preciseness of the time here, exactly a year, helps to highlight the difference between then and now.

> **▉ Remember**
>
> The term 'archaic' was defined earlier in this chapter. An **archaism** is a word used to suggest an earlier time.

4 Once we establish that the poem revolves around this difference in time, we can begin to explore what exactly is different in his reception, and wonder why. Is it the narrator who has changed, or the public? Although he says he has committed 'misdeeds', this may be ironic – it could be how the public perceives what he has done.

Titles of poems are usually highly significant. If we consider that the narrator a year ago was 'a patriot', but now he is to be hanged, could it be that it is the public who have changed, not him? That we send men off to fight, and at first glorify what they do, but when they return we want nothing to do with them?

Summary

This chapter has explored the significance of time in stories. In the representational world of stories, time needs to be compressed and altered. Looking at how authors do this, and to what effect, should be central to the way you analyse your chosen set texts. Looking at the significance of time and chronology will take you to the very heart of what the author is doing and the meanings that are being made.

4 | Characters and characterisation

Aims of the chapter:

- ▥ Establishes the importance of characters in stories.

- ▥ Explains that people in stories can have various levels of significance.

- ▥ Shows that all people in stories are there for a specific purpose.

▥ Key terms

Characterisation: the way in which an author creates and uses characters, and why.

▥ Activity 1

Below are some more names created by Dickens. Put them into two lists, one for good characters and one for bad. Then have a guess at what characteristic might be implied by the name of each character.

Thomas Gradgrind

Mr McChoakumchild

Stephen Blackpool

Josiah Bounderby

Charles Cheeryble

Sir Leicester Dedlock

Uriah Heep

Krook

Seth Pecksniff

Wackford Squeers

Miss Flite

Noddy Boffin

Esther Summerson

Ada Clare

▥ People in stories

Stories are about people doing things and having things done to them. (There are sometimes stories, especially those written for children, where animals replace people, but they still have distinctly human qualities.) When looking at aspects of narrative, though, you are not concerned with the characters as such, but with aspects of **characterisation**. Reminding yourself that a character is not real, does not actually exist outside the confines of the novel or poem, reminds you that you are looking at how authors achieve effects.

This not to say that as keen readers we do not lose ourselves in a book, and talk and think about characters as though they are real. But that reality is an illusion, a **representation** of people rather than the people themselves. Studying literature is not the same as just reading it – in studying literature you need to analyse rather than describe.

🔍 ⓘ Starting with a name

One of the first things we are given after we are born is a name: in our own culture the first part of an individual's name is a choice our parents make from a limited collection; the second part is a family name. Most of us have no choice about this and quite a few of us wish we could change what we have been given. Although the names we have can tell quite a bit about our cultural origins, it feels as though there is something random about what we end up with.

Fig. 1 *One of the Dickens characters listed in Activity 1. Which one do you think it is? For the answer, see the end of this chapter (p35)*

Link

For a Commentary on Activity 1, see the end of this chapter (p34).

There is nothing random, though, about the names of characters in literature, because of course they do not really exist. They have been invented by the author, and this offers the author a chance to signal to the reader what sort of person the character is. Names can carry a great deal of significance, in the process saving the author a lot of time and work. There are varying degrees of subtlety in this, depending in part on the genre of the text, but look closely and it is possible to see something significant in even the most ordinary of names – the ordinariness itself sometimes carrying significance.

The process of signification, though, is a cultural one. In other words, the meanings and associations we find in names are not there as of right; they are implied by the author and understood by those readers who have enough knowledge of the culture to make the connections. So when you read a fictional text that comes from a culture other than your own, you may miss the significance of all sorts of things, without necessarily losing the point of the text altogether. Two obvious ways that cultural references can be lost are through geography and through time. Texts from countries we are not fully familiar with, and texts from earlier times, require a special effort when reading, and an understanding on our part that we may not quite be getting the whole point.

AQA Examiner's tip

Never write about people in stories as though they are real. The more you can mention the author when talking about characters in texts, the better: this means that you will be writing about the characteristics people are given by authors, and how authors establish these characteristics.

One author who created a huge cast of characters was Charles Dickens. He often created names that were memorable (important in a complex plot) and at the same time pinned down the character to a certain physical or emotional characteristic. So, for example Silas Wegg (in *Our Mutual Friend*) has a wooden leg and is unpleasantly devious and greedy. While there is no reason in principle why a character called Silas Wegg could not be heroic, it somehow seems unlikely that an author would give a hero such a name.

Making an appearance

You have seen above that a fictional name can say a great deal about a fictional person. The same goes for the appearance of characters: what they look like, how they dress, their physical gestures, and so on. Characters in fictional texts are usually described early on, as part of the **establishment** of the text. Obviously in novels there is plenty of space to do this, whereas in narrative poems a couple of features are often enough to pin down not just what a character looks like, but what a character is like in a broader sense. Just as a name can conjure up ideas about a character's moral qualities, so can a description of their appearance.

Key terms

Establishment: refers to how texts begin, the work the author does for the reader at the beginning of the text. Establishment can involve introducing people, places, time, etc.

Activity 2

Look at the description below of the Mayor of Hamelin in Robert Browning's poem *The Pied Piper of Hamelin*. Based on these lines alone, what can you work out about the characteristics that he may show later in the story?

Did you know?

Hamelin is a town in Lower Saxony, Germany, best known for the events narrated in Browning's poem, which took place in medieval times and are re-enacted every Sunday throughout the summer as a tourist attraction.

(With the Corporation as he sat,
Looking little though wondrous fat;
Nor brighter was his eye, nor moister
Than a too-long-opened oyster,
Save at noon when his paunch grew mutinous
For a plate of turtle green and glutinous)

Robert Browning, The Pied Piper of Hamelin, *1842*

Commentary on Activity 2

There are a number of suggestions here that can be taken from this short extract, based upon the fact that authors often use **cultural stereotypes** as a short route to creating meanings. Here are the physical features that Browning describes:

Stature – small but fat

Eyes – dull and dry

Stomach – noisy when hungry, wanting glutinous food

It would be strange if any reader found this description anything other than repulsive, and a repulsive outside, in literary texts, often means an unpleasant 'inside' too. Browning here prepares us for the fact that the Mayor is both greedy and untrustworthy. Why untrustworthy? Because of his eyes, the eyes always being a key part of a character's description, carrying considerable significance beyond their literal description.

We have noticed above the importance of cultural significance. In many cultures the physical description involved in eyes and seeing comes to represent the internal process of knowing and understanding. In English, to say 'I can see' carries both the external and internal sense of the word. No wonder then that literature is full of references to eyes and seeing, especially when the eyes are also seen as 'the window to the soul'. The dull and dry eyes of the Mayor represent a man of little vision.

Key terms

Cultural stereotype: used here to suggest that authors present characters with features that we are conditioned to recognise as having a certain meaning. Bright eyes, for example, will often suggest wisdom and creativity.

It is an ancient Mariner,
And he stoppeth one of three.
'By thy long grey beard and glittering eye,
Now wherefore stopp'st thou me?

The Bridegroom's doors are opened wide,
And I am next of kin;
The guests are met, the feast is set:
May'st hear the merry din.'

He holds him with his skinny hand,
'There was ship,' quoth he.
Hold off! Unhand me, grey-beard loon!'
Eftsoons his hand dropt he.

He holds him with his glittering eye –
The Wedding-Guest stood still,
And listens like a three years' child:
The Mariner hath his will.

The Wedding-Guest sat on a stone:
He cannot choose but hear;
And thus spake on that ancient man,
The bright-eyed Mariner.

Samuel Taylor Coleridge,
The Rime of the Ancient Mariner, 1798

Activity 3

Look at the opening verses of Samuel Taylor Coleridge's narrative poem *The Rime of the Ancient Mariner*. What details about the appearance of the Ancient Mariner are given here? What do they suggest about him as a character?

Commentary on Activity 3

The Ancient Mariner has a long grey beard (signifying age), and a skinny hand (signifying age, but also perhaps a life devoid of pleasures such as food). But it is again the eyes that are most highlighted. They are mentioned three times: 'glittering eye' is mentioned twice and 'bright-eyed' once. It would appear that his eyes belie his physical appearance. He may be old and decrepit but inside he burns fiercely in his desire to endlessly tell his story. He is a man possessed by a mission.

■ **Activity 4**

Look at the paragraphs below which introduce the boy Hassan. Based on these descriptions, what can you work out about the characteristics that the author is establishing?

■ **Did you know?**

Khaled Hosseini was born in Afghanistan and moved to the USA in 1980. *The Kite Runner* was his first novel.

■ **Link**

For more on eye-dialect, see Chapter 2.

■ Characters in novels

As we saw above, novels can take a more leisurely look at appearance, especially when an important character is being portrayed. The example below is taken from Khaled Hosseini's novel *The Kite Runner*. Near the start of the novel the narrator, Amir, looks back to his childhood and begins to build up a picture of his friend Hassan, who is the Kite Runner of the title. Hassan is the son of a family servant, but a playmate of Amir. Later in the novel Amir betrays his friend, an action that lives with him for the rest of his life.

> I can still see Hassan up on that tree, sunlight flickering through the leaves on his almost perfect round face, a face like a Chinese doll chiseled from hardwood: his flat, broad nose and slanting, narrow eyes like bamboo leaves, eyes that looked, depending on the light, gold, green, even sapphire. I can still see his tiny low-set ears and that pointed stub of a chin, a meaty appendage that looked like it was added as a mere afterthought. And the cleft lip, just left of mid-line, where the Chinese doll maker's instrument may have slipped, or perhaps he had simply grown tired and careless.
>
> Sometimes, up in those trees, I talked Hassan into firing walnuts with his slingshot at the neighbour's one-eyed German shepherd. Hassan never wanted to, but if I asked, *really* asked, he wouldn't deny me. Hassan never denied me anything.

Khaled Hosseini, The Kite Runner, 2003, pp3–4

Commentary on Activity 4

Unlike the description of the Mayor in the poem above, this time we are meant to form a positive picture of the character. His face is 'almost perfect' and there is a sense here that the slight imperfection, the lip, makes him even more attractive. The eyes are again given prominence, but this time they shine, with not one colour but three. The poetic comparison, the way the boy is in harmony with his surroundings, is also a hint that here is someone special by character if not by social status.

Hassan's loyalty to his friend is then shown, which takes on much greater significance once we know that his friend will betray him.

🔍 It's how you say it

Obviously what characters have to say is of huge importance to how a text works, but authors can also signal aspects of character by giving their creations distinctive speech manners, or mannerisms. Sometimes these can be used to represent social class: working-class characters, for example, might be given a certain identity through the use of **eye-dialect**, thus linking character with setting and place.

In the following example the effect is rather more subtle, with the speech going against what we might initially expect. In this extract from a poem by Browning, the speaker has actually murdered his wife.

Here, in monologue form, the speaker of the poem *My Last Duchess* talks about the woman he has killed, while looking at a painting of her. He is speaking within the poem to an employee of the family who are going to provide the next Duchess.

Oh sir, she smiled, no doubt,
Whene'er I passed her; but who passed without
Much the same smile? This grew; I gave commands;
Then all smiles stopped together. There she stands
As if alive. Will't please you rise? We'll meet
The company below, then. I repeat,
The Count your master's known munificence
Is ample warrant that no pretence
Of mine for dowry will be disallowed;
Though his fair daughter's self, as I avowed
At starting, is my object.

Robert Browning, My Last Duchess, *1842*

Browning here uses the speaker's voice to alert the hearer/reader outside the text to the appalling nature of this character. The formal words, some linked to money – 'munificence', 'ample warrant' – do not mask the fact that this insanely jealous man, who could not bear his wife to smile at anyone but himself, is currently undertaking another business venture to do the same to his next wife. And even more scary is that he is not interrupted.

Browning also uses the condensed form of poetry to chilling effect. Look how much is packed into the following lines, with the suggestion that it is all of the same importance to the speaker, who of course knows what he has done to the last duchess.

There she stands
As if alive. Will't please you rise? We'll meet
The company below, then.

The ins and outs of characterisation

So far you have seen three ways of creating characters, all of which are external: names, physical appearance and speech habits. You have also seen that poetry, which often works in briefer and more symbolic ways, makes particular use of these short cuts.

There are, though, other ways in which characters are presented, some of which are also external, and some of which are more to do with the internal workings of the characters – their thoughts and motives. Again, the poem can do less with these than the novel, which is not necessarily a drawback. Hinting at thoughts and motives, rather than following them carefully, can create an unsettling effect.

Activity 5

Below is a list of some of the ways in which characters can be presented by author – in other words, some of the ways in which we get to know about a character. As you consider this list, see if you agree with the external/internal labels that have been attached. Is anything missing from the list?

How the character is named	external
What the character looks like	external
The character's speech habits	external
What the character does, their actions	external
The character's motives for what they do	internal
What the character has to say	external/internal
What the character thinks	internal
What others says about the character	external/internal
What others think about the character	internal/external

There is no commentary on this activity.

AQA Examiner's tip

Do not take dialogue and speech for granted. They can tell you a great deal about how the story is being constructed and shaped.

Link

The last four aspects listed in Activity 5 lead to the next chapter, which looks at voices in texts.

■ Link: extract 12

To complete Activity 6 you will need to use *The Patriot* which is printed in the Extracts section at the back of this book, extract 12.

■ *The Patriot*

As in previous chapters, we conclude by looking at *The Patriot*.

■ Activity 6

This chapter has looked at some of the ways authors use external features of characterisation, such as naming, appearance, actions, to develop their stories. Now look again at *The Patriot* and answer the following questions:

1 What people are included in the poem?

2 What external clues are given to the identity of these people?

3 Are actions important in this poem?

■ Extension tasks

1 Consider the novels that you are studying, and discuss the following issues:

- Can you find significance in the way any of the characters are named?
- Can you find any significance in the way characters are described externally? This need not be limited to their physical characteristics, but could also include the jobs they do etc.
- Are any of the characters given any noticeable features of speech that help you to remember them and their specific traits?
- Are there any other aspects of the author's methods of characterisation that you can identify?

2 Consider the poetry texts that you are studying, and discuss the following issues:

- To what extent do the poems show aspects of individual characters?
- What methods does the poet use to create characters?
- Does the speaker of the poem have a discernible character? If so, how is it created?

■ Commentaries

Commentary on Activity 1

Good

Esther Summerson, (because of summer)

Ada Clare (sweetness)

Noddy Boffin (eccentricity)

Miss Flite (lightness?)

Charles Cheeryble (humour)

Stephen Blackpool (more open to question, but solid and dependable)

Bad

Thomas Gradgrind (hard-sounding)

Mr McChoakumchild (a teacher – as it says!)

Josiah Bounderby (cad)

Uriah Heep (a creep)

Krook (a thief)

Seth Pecksniff (two unpleasant words together)

Sir Leicester Dedlock (intransigent and unmoveable)

Wackford Squeers (a different kind of teacher)

Illustration of Dickens character

The illustration is of Uriah Heep, from David Copperfield.

Commentary on Activity 6

1 There is the patriot himself who narrates the poem, and the people of the city.

2 The patriot has a label: he is 'The Patriot', but has no name. The people of the city are described a year ago, when they are enthusiastic about what The Patriot is doing, but now they are absent, waiting offstage somewhere else to see him hanged. Only 'a palsied few' remain in the town itself, presumably because they cannot move.

3 Actions are implied rather than seen. In his year away The Patriot has lived life to the full – 'Naught man could do, have I left undone' – but we are given no actual details about whether this refers to public actions in war, or more private actions.

Summary

This chapter has looked at some of the ways in which people in texts are created and given characteristics. The focus has been on some of the external methods of characterisation, and your attention has been drawn to some of the differences between poetry and novels.

Voices in texts

Aims of the chapter:

■ Explains the different kinds
of voices in texts: characters
and narrator.

■ Shows ways of identifying
the different voices in texts.

The idea of voices in texts is closely linked to the aspect of characters
and characterisation discussed in the previous chapter. Voices in texts
can be the actual 'voices' of characters who get to speak in the text, and
they can also be the thoughts of characters and the voice of the narrator.
Identifying voices in texts can be a complicated business, but at AS-
level there are some basic issues to understand which will help you
think about how narratives work. In the real world, we can shut out the
extraneous noise of people talking, and we certainly cannot hear people
think. In fictional worlds, when somebody talks we take notice, and
sometimes we can also access what they are thinking.

Direct speech and attribution

Activity 1

Look at the following extract from *Small Island* by Andrea Levy. Here
Hortense, newly arrived in London from Jamaica in 1948 and accompanied
by her landlady Mrs Bligh, tells of going to buy some food. The first person to
speak is the shopkeeper, who has red hair.

1   How many speaking voices can you identify in this extract?

2   What information relating to their speech is given in addition to the
actual words they say? Is this significant?

'What can I do you for?' he asked me directly. A red Englishman!
　　'He wants to know if you'd like anything,' Mrs Bligh told me.
　　I obliged her concern by making a purchase. 'A tin of condensed
milk, please,' I asked him.
　　But this red man stared back at me as if I had not uttered the
words. No light of comprehension sparkled in his eye. 'I beg your
pardon?' he said.
　　Condensed milk, I said, five times, and still he looked on me
bewildered. Why no one in this country understand my English? At
college my diction was admired by all. I had to point at the wretched
tin of condensed milk, which resided just behind his head.
　　'Oh, condensed milk,' he told me, as if I had not been saying it
all along.
　　Tired of this silly dance of incomprehension, I did not bother to
ask for the loaf of bread – I just point to the bread on the counter.

Andrea Levy, Small Island, 2004, pp331–2

Commentary on Activity 1

1   Three people's words are quoted here, in what we call **direct speech**.
The speakers are the unnamed shopkeeper, Mrs Bligh and Hortense
herself.

2   Every time someone speaks their contribution is **attributed**. So for the
first three speeches we get:

Key terms

Direct speech: the actual words
spoken by characters in a
narrative.

Attributed: describes direct speech
that is identified (i.e. the reader is
told who is speaking).

▨ he asked me directly

▨ Mrs Bligh told me

▨ I asked him.

Note that a variety of words can be used to attribute speech instead of the straightforward 'said'. Are they just used to give variety? Possibly, but to be 'told' something might indicate that you are being treated as an inferior. In addition, if the attribution includes *how* someone speaks, then further information is given. The shopkeeper 'asked directly'. Does that hint at a certain rudeness perhaps, especially as he has made a sort of joke?

There is also, though, another voice in the text, 'speaking' to the reader. Because the narrative is **first person**, we can confidently say that voice belongs to Hortense, not speaking *in* the story but speaking *in the telling of* the story.

If we want to make this a little more complicated, we can find her using a range of voices. Sometimes she tells the story, at other times she reflects on its significance to her at the time of the event. So in the line:

> Condensed milk, I said, five times, and still he looked on me bewildered

we have Hortense telling the story. However, in the line

> Why no one in this country understand my English?

Hortense is *thinking* about what is happening and trying to find a reason. This thought, though, is not attributed: it is **free**. The fact that she thinks in a slightly non-British standard form of English adds to our awareness that she is not being understood by others in the story, but she is of course being understood by us the readers.

What we have seen in the activity above is that speaking and thinking can both lead to 'voices', and that sometimes these voices are attributed and sometimes free. An example of free speech from the same novel is given below. Here Hortense, recently arrived in England, talks to her husband who has lived there for some time. Hortense speaks first – an important point when you are having to follow a sequence without being told who is speaking:

> 'Who is that woman downstairs?'…
> 'Oh, Queenie – she own the house.'
> 'You know her?'
> 'Of course. She own the house. She is the landlady.'
> 'She married?'
> 'Her husband lost in the war.'
> 'She on her own?'
> 'Yes.'
> 'You friendly with her?'

Andrea Levy, Small Island, *2004, pp28–9*

Sometimes writers use free speech to give variety, maybe to hurry the action a bit. The effect of this stretch of free speech is more specific, though: it sounds very much as though Hortense is suspicious of her husband and is conducting some sort of interrogation. (There comes a point with free speech, incidentally, when the reader can lose track – we are all familiar with having to go back to the beginning to work out who is talking.)

▨ **Remember**

A first-person narrative is a story told through the voice of one of the characters, using 'I', as opposed to a third-person narrative in which the story is told by a narrator who is not one of the characters.

▨ **Key terms**

Free: in a technical sense, describes thought or speech that is not attributed (i.e. the reader is not told specifically who is speaking or thinking).

AQA **Examiner's tip**

It is well worth using some of the technical terms defined above when analysing the ways in which authors create speaking and thinking voices. The terminology is not essential, but it helps you to deal with the analysis quickly and accurately.

▮ Indirect speech

In addition to giving the actual words spoken, a narrator can report what was said in what we call **indirect speech**. An example from *Small Island* is given below. This time the narrator is Mrs Bligh, whose neighbour and her husband have objected to Mrs Bligh having a black lodger.

💡 Activity 2

Read the extract below and answer the following questions:

1. Identify the direct speech.
2. Identify the indirect speech.
3. For the indirect speech write out a direct speech version.
4. Is there any thought presented here?

> But Blanche, or Mrs Smith as she now wanted me to call her, put her house up for sale. Furious with me. Told me it wasn't so much her as her husband. 'This is not what he wanted, Mrs Bligh. He's just back from fighting a war and now this country no longer feels his own.' What was it all for? That's what it left Morris wondering. And she told me she had her two little girls' welfare to think of.

Andrea Levy, Small Island, 2004, p117

Commentary on Activity 2

1. There is one piece of direct speech, the sentences beginning 'This is not what he wanted....'. We are helped in identifying this by the use of **speech marks**; although they are the traditional way of marking direct speech, in modern novels they are not always used.

2 and 3 Indirect speech is as follows, with a possible direct speech version following:

> *Mrs Smith as she now wanted me to call her*
> 'I want you to call me Mrs Smith'

> *Furious with me*
> 'I am furious with you'

> *Told me it was not so much her as her husband*
> 'It's not me, it is my husband', she told me.

> *What was it all for? That's what it left Morris wondering.*
> 'Morris has been left wondering what it is all for.'

> *And she told me she had her two little girls' welfare to think of*
> 'I have my two little girls' welfare think of', she told me.

4. There are a few structural points to note here. Note that pronouns and verb tenses change when moving from direct to indirect speech, as does word order. Also, note, it is possible to have **attributed** indirect speech and **free** indirect speech. Where the indirect speech is free, it merges seamlessly into the narrative. The same goes for indirect free thought. The sentence 'Furious with me' has been assumed to be spoken in the list above, but it could be thought only – Mrs Bligh's interpretation of her neighbour's words, rather than the actual words being spoken. The use of free indirect thought and speech allows authors to create a certain ambiguity when telling the story.

So what is gained by using indirect speech? Well again, in the long run, authors will use it for variety. Here, though, it may serve another purpose: in not being given many of Mrs Smith's actual words, they are being downgraded, rendered less powerful.

To recap on what we have found so far: one way in which we get information in a story is through what we are 'told' by characters involved. Areas to consider include:

▨ Who speaks, to whom and when?

▨ What are they talking about?

▨ What information does the talk give (a) other characters and (b) the reader?

▨ Is the speech direct or indirect?

▨ Is the speech attributed or free?

▨ If attributed, is the attitude towards the character contained in the attribution?

▨ Whose thoughts are accessed?

▨ Are these thoughts attributed or free?

▨ Voices in stories can help to establish character traits, and so are part of **characterisation**, but they also enable authors to provide information.

Although there are always exceptions to every rule in literature, it is largely true to say that novels do not provide the so-called small talk that is such a feature of our everyday 'real' lives. This is because narrative is about information, and small talk, while being very important socially, does not tell a story as such.

▨ Thought in novels

One of the distinctive features of the novel form is that it can give us the detailed thoughts of characters as the story progresses. This is possible up to a point in poetry, but much more problematic in drama, where artificial means have to be used if characters are going to 'speak' their thoughts. The fact that the novel as a form allows thought to be given makes it interestingly different from real life: in real life we can think ourselves but cannot access the thoughts of others unless they choose to give us a version of them. Not surprisingly, novelists make full use of thoughts to give their characters distinctive voices and so character traits.

In Chapter 3 we saw the opening action of Ian McEwan's *Enduring Love*. Soon after the event, where a boy is eventually rescued in the balloon accident but a man dies, the first-person narrator of the novel, Joe Rose, reflects on what had happened the previous day. This is done by the use of indirect thought, so we do not get the actual words he thought and speech marks are not used.

▨ Link

Reread the extract from *Enduring Love* in Chapter 3 to remind yourself of what happened there.

▨ Activity 3

Read the extract below and answer the following questions:

1 Identify the points where McEwan makes it clear that Joe is thinking here.

2 What do you notice about the references to time near the beginning of the extract?

3 What contribution to the novel as a whole might this extract be serving? Think in terms of the characterisation of Joe and the issues raised by what he thinks.

I had left Clarissa sleeping and brought with me my coffee, the paper and my pages from the night before.

But instead of reading myself or others I thought about John Logan and how we had killed him. Yesterday the events of the day before had dimmed. This morning the blustery sunshine illumined and animated the whole tableau. I could feel the rope in my hands again as I examined the welts. I made calculations. If Gadd had stayed in the basket with his grandson, and if the rest of us had hung on, and if we assumed an average weight of a hundred and sixty pounds each, then surely eight hundred pounds would have kept us close to the ground. If the first person had not let go, then surely the rest of us would have stayed in place. And who was this first person? Not me. Not me. I even said the words aloud. I remembered a plummeting mass and the sudden upward jerk of the balloon. But I could not tell whether this mass was in front of me, or to my left or right. If I knew the position, I would know the person.

Could this person be blamed? As I drank my coffee the rush hour below began its slow crescendo. It was hard to think this through. Phrases, well-worn and counter-weighted, occurred to me, resolving nothing. On the one hand, the first pebble in an avalanche, and on the other, the breaking of ranks. The cause, but not the morally responsible agent. The scales tipping, from altruism to self-interest. Was it panic, or rational calculation? Had we killed him really, or simply refused to die with him? But if we had been with him, stayed with him, no one would have died.

Ian McEwan, Enduring Love, *pp55–6*

Commentary on Activity 3

1   McEwan makes it clear at various points that Joe is thinking rather than speaking (although there is one point where he speaks to himself – an advanced form of thinking perhaps!). We are given the following attributions as part of indirect thought:

> I thought
> I could feel
> I remembered
> It was hard to think this through
> Occurred to me.

It could also be argued that the many question marks also signify a thought process.

2   The references to time at the beginning of the extract are as follows:

> the night before
> yesterday
> this morning.

They show a subtle shift from a distant past (*the night before* instead of *last night*) to a more recent past (*yesterday* instead of *the previous day* and *this morning* instead of *that morning*). This subtle shift brings the thought processes a little closer to the reader.

3   In terms of its wider contribution this extract establishes certain character traits which can be seen in Joe. He is considerate and concerned, worried about the accident and its causes. He is also very rational, teasing out reasons for what had happened. We are also meant to see him as an intelligent man, whose thoughts, as given

to us here, sound like formal writing. Although all thoughts in a novel are written down, authors can try to represent them in various ways as more random and chaotic than those given here. Even the questions, which in part represent the flow of ideas, also suggest a questioning of events in a scientific way.

What we see here, then, is that thought can be as significant as talk in helping an author tell a story. Add thought to talk and action and you have three of the key ingredients to storytelling and narrative.

Third-person narrative

In the extract from *Enduring Love* we have seen an example of how thought can be used within a first-person narrative. It can also be used within third-person narratives, and often with a wider frame of reference: a third-person narrative can access a much wider number of characters and their thoughts, and in the process shift the point of view. Where free thought is used, it can also form part of the overall narrative, making it difficult to see whether it is a character's thoughts we are being given, in which case the information is open to question, or whether it is the voice of the more authoritative narrator.

In real life, of course, there is no narrator to oversee our thoughts and actions. In a philosophical sense there is no definitive truth about something, only the aggregation of all our thoughts and words on it. So if the owner of a house thinks it looks lovely from the outside and a passer-by thinks it looks tatty, we cannot say that either is right. Modern novelists in particular work with the idea that there cannot be absolute truths, only the words, thoughts and actions of people, and they try to reflect this lack of certainty in their novels.

Anne Tyler does this in her novel *Digging to America*. Although the novel is technically written in the third person, we soon work out that each chapter is very much driven by the thoughts of one particular character through the use of **indirect free thought**.

Using the idea that is given above of how a house looks, the extract begins with the following sentence:

> The Donaldsons' house was a worn white clapboard Colonial on one of the narrower streets in Mount Washington.

There are two words here which alert the reader that this might not be a definitive description from an unbiased narrator, but could belong to a character instead. Describing the house as 'worn' suggests a potential criticism, as does the statement that the Donaldsons lived in one of the 'narrower' streets. Although this could just be the narrator giving straight description, it could also be what one of the characters thinks about the Donaldsons – that they are not quite as posh as they think they are.

We will now look at the full extract, which needs some context to make sense. Previously in the novel, two families have adopted Korean girls and brought them to America. The Donaldsons are an all-American family, the Yazdans are Iranian Americans. The two families first met when the children arrived at the airport, and now they are about to meet again for the first time since then. Jim and Bitsy Donaldson have called their adopted daughter Jin-ho; Sami and Ziba Yazdan have called theirs Susan (note the names here). Maryam is Sami's mother, and it is her thoughts that dominate this extract.

Link

See Chapter 6 for a discussion of point of view.

Hint

See the definitions of the key terms **indirect speech** and **free** earlier in this chapter if you are not sure what indirect free thought is.

The Donaldsons' house was a worn white clapboard Colonial on one of the narrower streets in Mount Washington. The sprawling, woodsy yard was ankle-deep in yellow leaves that clattered as the Yazdans waded up the front walk, and the porch was strewn with bicycles and boots and garden tools. It was Brad who opened the door, wearing corduroys and a woolen shirt stretched taut across his belly. 'Well, hey!' he said. 'Welcome! Great to see you!' and he chucked Susan under the chin. 'This kid has plumped up some. She was looking a bit peaked at the airport.'

'Fifteen pounds, three ounces, at her last doctor visit,' Ziba told him.

'Fifteen?' He frowned.

'And three ounces.'

'I guess she's going to be one of those *petite* little people,' he said.

Jin-Ho was going to be an Amazon, Maryam thought when she saw her straddling Bitsy's waist. She was stocky and bloomingly healthy-looking, with fat cheeks and bright, laughing eyes. She still wore that squared-off hairstyle she had arrived with, seemingly all of a piece, and although she too was in corduroys, her top was a multicolored, quilted affair with striped sleeves and a black silk sash – the kind of thing Maryam recalled from the days when Sami and Ziba were researching Korea. 'Hasn't she grown?' Bitsy asked, shifting Jin-Ho slightly to give everyone a good view. 'These pants are size eighteen months! We had to switch her to a full crib the second week she was here.'

Bitsy herself wore a black-and-white-striped jersey and black slacks and fluorescent jogging shoes. There was something aggressive about her plainness, Maryam thought – her blatant lack of makeup, her chopped hair and angular, rawboned body. She might almost be making a statement. Next to her, Ziba looked very glamorous but also a little bit flashy.

Anne Tyler, Digging to America, *pp22–3*

Commentary on Activity 4

1 We know that we are being given this information via Maryam's thoughts because sometimes we are specifically told this, as in 'Jin-Ho was going to be an Amazon, Maryam thought…'. When Tyler does this she is using indirect thought – that is, not the actual thoughts but a reported version of them. This happens three times: twice with 'Maryam thought' and once with 'Maryam recalled'. Note here that just as speech can be attributed with many more words than 'she said', so there are various words that can replace 'she thought', such as 'she recalled' as used here, but also 'she wondered', 'she reflected' and so on.

2 We have already seen Maryam being critical of the Donaldsons' house. Other potential points of criticism include:

The unswept leaves
Brad's belly
Jin-Ho's size
Bitsy's appearance
Ziba being a bit flashy.

The fact that Maryam is critical of others, and by implication of Americans and their diets, adds a dimension to her characterisation, showing once again that the building blocks of narrative work very much together to achieve their effects.

3 Because the Donaldsons' thoughts are not being accessed here we can only get their views from direct speech, from what they say. So they seem critical of Susan's smallness, and later on they boast about Jin-Ho's physical growth, implying perhaps that she is more developed than Susan in all sorts of ways.

The overall effect of the narrative here is to give humour – humour at the competition between the families, humour at different cultural values and also potential humour at Maryam's bias and willingness to criticise, which we as readers can see through, provided we detect the way the narrative is working. The humour, though, is social and observational – there is nothing biting here as all the characters are essentially decent people.

Voices in poetry

Narrative poems too have voices within them that help tell the story. How many voices, and what use is made of the voices, can vary, though. Some of the narrative poems in your AS course selection are quite short, and so are likely to have fewer voices than the extended narrative poems which are another option.

Activity 5

The following extracts have already been seen in previous chapters. For each one, identify:

- how many voices there are
- whether the voice presents speaking or thinking
- whether the voices are attributed or free
- what effects the poet is achieving through using voices in this way.

Link

For each poem in Activity 5 there is a short commentary at the end of this chapter (p45).

1 The Rime of the Ancient Mariner (opening lines)

It is an ancient Mariner,
And he stoppeth one of three.
'By thy long grey beard and glittering eye,
Now wherefore stopp'st thou me?

The Bridegroom's doors are opened wide,
And I am next of kin;
The guests are met, the feast is set:
May'st hear the merry din.'

He holds him with his skinny hand,
'There was ship,' quoth he.
'Hold off! Unhand me, grey-beard loon!'
Eftsoons his hand dropt he.

Samuel Taylor Coleridge

2 O What Is That Sound? (opening lines)

O what is that sound which so thrills the ear
Down in the valley drumming, drumming?
Only the scarlet soldiers, dear,
The soldiers coming.

O what is that light I see flashing so clear
Over the distance brightly, brightly?
Only the sun on their weapons, dear,
As they step lightly.

W.H. Auden

3 Godiva (opening lines)

I waited for the train at Coventry;
I hung with grooms and porters on the bridge,
To watch the three tall spires; and there I shaped
The city's ancient legend into this:

Not only we, the latest seed of Time,
New men, that in the flying of a wheel
Cry down the past, not only we, that prate
Of rights and wrongs, have loved the people well,
And loathed to see them overtax'd; but she
Did more, and underwent, and overcame,
The woman of a thousand summers back,
Godiva, wife to that grim Earl, who ruled
In Coventry: for when he laid a tax
Upon his town, and all the mothers brought
Their children, clamoring, 'If we pay, we starve!'
She sought her lord, and found him, where he strode
About the hall, among his dogs, alone,
His beard a foot before him and his hair
A yard behind. She told him of their tears,
And pray'd him, 'If they pay this tax, they starve.'
Whereat he stared, replying, half-amazed,
'You would not let your little finger ache
For such as these?' – 'But I would die,' said she.

Alfred Tennyson

The Patriot

Link: extract 12

To complete Activity 6 you will need to use *The Patriot* which is printed in the Extracts section at the back of this book, extract 12.

Activity 6

This chapter has looked at some of the ways authors use voices in narratives. Now look again at *The Patriot* and answer the following question:

- What voices are in the poem and how are they presented?

Extension tasks

1 Consider the novels that you are studying. Choose a representative section (say a chapter) and discuss the following issues:

- How is speech used in this chapter of the novel?
- Is attribution used to indicate aspects of character?
- Is thought given in this chapter? Whose thoughts are given?
- Are there points in the chapter where who is speaking/thinking is deliberately ambiguous?

2 Consider the poetry texts that you are studying, and discuss the following issues:

- To what extent do the poems contain direct speech? What is the effect of this?
- Do the poems have a range of speakers?
- Who is heard and who is not? Is this significant?

Commentaries

Commentary on Activity 5

1 The Rime of the Ancient Mariner

There are three voices: the narrator, the Mariner and the Wedding-Guest. It would seem that all voices are spoken rather than thought. The Wedding-Guest's speech is free (so in fact more than one guest could be speaking). The Mariner's is attributed. Coleridge establishes right at the start that this is a narrative poem with a mix of narrative and speech. It is also dramatic and rather strange.

2 O What Is That Sound?

Here there are two free voices, each speaker signalled by a different font. The fact that they are not attributed means we do not know who they are, creating a deliberate ambiguity – they could be any people under threat from forces of repression at any time.

3 Godiva

There are three direct speaking voices here, all attributed. They are the poor mothers, Lady Godiva and her husband. The fact that they are all attributed means that Tennyson's method is different from Auden's. He wants to be clear about the specifics and tells the story conventionally, even if it is probably in fact a legend.

The other voice is the first-person narrator, which, because of the opening time frame, seems like a representation of Tennyson himself. Whether this is thought or spoken is not clear; nor is who it is addressed to.

Commentary on Activity 6

The dominant voice is that of The Patriot, who sounds as though he is making a final speech before his execution. The voice is resigned and thoughtful rather than aggressive and angry, which presumably it could be, given his treatment.

There is one other brief piece of reported speech, the collective 'cries' of the people celebrating his return. There are also some short pieces of direct speech, but they are slightly different from others we have seen. Within the world of this story they are not words that have been spoken, they are words that might have been spoken. So in the first instance he pretends to ask for the impossible and the grateful crowd willing to give him anything. This make-believe exchange heightens the sense of love and gratitude that the people have for their hero.

The second imaginary piece of direct speech involves God, who makes the moral point that earthly riches are nothing compared with eternal ones.

Summary

This chapter has looked at some of the ways in which authors use speaking and thinking voices in texts. One result of this process has been to see that it contributes to the point of view of the story, an idea that is developed further in the next chapter.

6 Points of view

Aims of the chapter:

- Explains that stories are told from certain viewpoints.
- Shows how these viewpoints are carefully managed by authors to convey meanings.
- Demonstrates that the words we use to explain how a story is told are the same words used to examine the ideas that the story presents.

Remember

Metaphor (a key term used in Chapter 2) involves the transfer of meaning, with one thing described as another (e.g. life is a journey).

Remember

The **ideology** of a text (a key term used in Chapter 1) is the attitudes, values and assumptions that the text contains.

Visual and spatial metaphors

The term **point of view** is very important when studying aspects of narrative, but it is hard to define, partly because it is a **metaphor** based upon a visual and spatial idea. If you are at a football match, and you stand behind the goal, that is your point of viewing the game. If you are on the side of the pitch, that is a different point of view, as is the view from the other end of the ground. And it can easily be argued that where you stand affects how you see the game. It depends upon your position, your standpoint. Behind the goal where your own team scores gives a different perspective from being at the far end of the pitch. Digital television coverage nowadays even allows you to change your angle in the living room.

So where, as readers, we are 'placed' in the telling of the story is vital to the way we interpret it, in just the same way as where we stand in the football ground affects how well we think our team has played.

While this football analogy should be clear, you may have noticed that in explaining point of view, other metaphorical terms were used, which also depend upon visual and spatial concepts. So we can say:

- It depends upon your point of view.
- It depends upon where you stand – your standpoint.
- It depends upon what perspective you take.
- It depends upon your position.
- It depends upon the angle you take.

These terms can have another level of meaning too. Here we are not just talking about your physical position, we are also talking about your position in terms of the beliefs you hold, ideas you have. To continue with the football analogy, we might say something like, 'whether or not Bobby Smith should be sacked as manager depends upon your point of view, but I think he's doing a good job'.

For our purposes, then, looking at point of view is important because it allows us to analyse narratives technically and also in terms of their ideas and views: how they see the world. Point of view is therefore both the technical description to do with how a text works and an indication of the **ideology** in a text. By exploring both these elements we are able to arrive at a more complete reading of the text.

Fig. 1 *Different points of view*

Link

See especially Chapter 5 for a discussion and examples of first- and third-person narratives.

The narrator – first person or third person?

We have already used the terms **first person** and **third person** in earlier chapters. They are the starting points for a more sophisticated way of looking at narratives, and as such it is useful to consider in a broad sense what they allow writers to do.

Activity 1

Imagine you are going to write a story about two people meeting and falling in love.

1 Consider telling it in the first person, through one of the two people meeting. What are the advantages and disadvantages of this?

2 Now consider telling it in the third person. What are the advantages and disadvantages of this?

3 Can you think of any other ways the story could be told?

Commentary on Activity 1

1 An advantage of the first-person method is that it can be intimate, close to the action, have a very personal narrative voice. But within this advantage lies a distinct disadvantage: the narrator can only report on what they themselves think and feel, and only on action that takes place when they are present. There are ways round this of course: other characters can tell you what they did, what they think, and you can use devices like letters, diaries, emails, and so on, to provide further information. There are times, though, when the narrator can seem almost required to be the novelist, to give the reader necessary information – and at times such as these the first-person method is at its least effective.

2 The advantage of the third-person narrative is that it offers the author the possibility of taking the narrative anywhere, of observing everything and everyone – but the downside is that this can feel quite remote to the reader and it can lack the personal nature of the first-person method.

3 In reality, authors do not necessarily have to stick rigidly to one method, and there are many ingenious ways to overcome narrative problems. For example, there can be more than one first-person narrator in a novel, with the switch clearly marked in the chapter headings. Or there can be a third-person narrative, but one that changes the point of view, often getting very close to different characters one at a time. Using **indirect free thought** can be a great help here.

99 Ways to Tell a Story

One way to understand how the narrative can shift across characters is to see this represented visually. In his comic book *99 Ways to Tell a Story*, Matt Madden tells the same story in 99 different pages of drawings. The first he calls 'Template', which is reproduced overleaf.

Link

See Chapter 5 for more on indirect free thought.

Activity 2

Look at 'Template' and answer the following questions:

1. Write out the story, frame by frame.

2. Now write out the plot using a third-person narrative.

3. What narrative methods that you have already learnt about (e.g. treatment of time, use of different voices) are used here?

Link

For a Commentary on Activity 2, see the end of this chapter (p53).

Fig. 2 *'Template'*

Activity 3

1. Now look at the same story but this time labelled 'Upstairs'. What extra information are we given by 'going upstairs'?

2. What are the crucial differences between this drawing and the previous one called 'Template'?

Link

For a Commentary on Activity 3, see the end of this chapter (p53).

Fig. 3 *'Upstairs'*

■ Proximity to the action

Another way in which the narrative point of view can be varied is by how close to the action we as readers are allowed to get. Is it viewed from a certain distance or is it viewed in close-up? What is our proximity? If you look at the Template drawing you will see that Madden uses a sort of zoom effect when the man's hand goes to the fridge door (frame 6). This is much closer to the action than frame 3, which seems the most distant.

■ Activity 4

Here are the opening sentences of each of the first five paragraphs of *Birdsong* by Sebastian Faulks. The novel begins in France in 1910. What do you notice about the focus of each of the paragraphs? How does each paragraph connect with the one before? The paragraphs have been numbered for ease of reference.

1   The boulevard du Cange was a broad, quiet street that marked the eastern flank of the city of Amiens. The wagons that rolled in from Lille and Arras to the north made directly into the tanneries and mills of the Saint-Leu quarter without needing to use this rutted, leafy road. The town side of the boulevard backed on to substantial gardens which were squared off and apportioned with civic precision to the houses they adjoined ...

2   Behind the gardens the river Somme broke up into small canals that were the picturesque feature of Saint-Leu; on the other side of the boulevard these had been made into a series of water-gardens, little islands of damp fertility divided by the channels of the split river ...

3   The Azaires' house showed a strong, formal front towards the road from behind iron railings. The traffic looping down towards the river would have been in no doubt that this was the property of a substantial man. ...

4   Inside, the house was both smaller and larger than it looked. It had no rooms of intimidating grandeur, no gilt ballrooms with dripping chandeliers, yet it had unexpected spaces and corridors that disclosed new corners with steps down into the gardens ...

5   Stephen Wraysford's metal trunk had been sent ahead and was waiting at the foot of the bed. He unpacked his clothes and hung his spare suit in the giant carved wardrobe ...

Sebastian Faulks, Birdsong, *pp3–4*

Commentary on Activity 4

In each paragraph the focus gets tighter, zooming in from a broad starting point and getting more and more specific. It goes something like this:

1   We see a quite distant view of a town, region, district and main street, followed by houses and gardens.

2   Then we get closer by seeing the already mentioned gardens and what lies behind them.

3   This is followed by a closer view, of a single house belonging to a well-off family.

4   Next we go inside the house, looking round in general.

5   And finally we go to a specific room inhabited by a specific man – clearly an Englishman who has come to stay, for an as yet unspecified reason.

Both distance and proximity can be useful: among other things distance can tend to let us judge characters and their actions, see the importance of places, while proximity will allow us to be more involved with characters, their relationships, their emotions.

Shifting perspectives

This chapter is headed 'Points of view', because perspectives frequently shift and move within texts – this is certainly the case in novels, but can be seen in poems too. Sometimes, to highlight the different perceptions of characters, and perhaps misunderstandings between them, essentially the same incident is seen twice, first from one character's point of view, then from another's. The following extracts from *Small Island* come early in the novel, when Hortense has arrived in London in 1948 from Jamaica, to be reunited with her husband Gilbert who has lived in London for some time – and has failed to meet her at the dock. Hortense has just seen the room they are to live in and is horrified at how small it is. Gilbert on the other hand, is aware that living in London means you live in small rooms. We, as readers, understand their misunderstanding in a way that the two characters do not.

 Activity 5

How does Andrea Levy show the differing perceptions of the two characters in each of the extracts? Can you see a third point of view here, which involves what the reader could think about this exchange?

Hortense

'Well,' I said, 'show me the rest, then, Gilbert'. The man just stared. 'Show me the rest, nah. I am tired from the long journey.' He scratched his head. 'The other rooms, Gilbert. The ones you busy making so nice for me you forgot to come to the dock.'

Gilbert spoke so softly I could hardly hear. He said, 'But this is it.'
'I am sorry?' I said.
'This is it, Hortense. This is the room I am living.'

Three steps would take me to one side of this room. Four steps could take me to another. There was a sink in the corner, a rusty tap stuck out from the wall above it. There was a table with two chairs – one with its back broken – pushed up against the bed. The armchair held a shopping bag, a pyjama top, and a teapot. In the fireplace the gas hissed with a blue flame.

'Just this?' I had to sit on the bed. My legs gave way. There was no bounce underneath me as I fell. 'Just this? This is where you are living? Just this?'

Gilbert

'Is this the way the English live?' How many times she ask me that question? I lose count. 'This the way the English live?' That question became a mournful lament, sighed on each and every thing she see. 'Is this the way the English live?'

'Yes', I tell her, 'this is the way the English live … there has been a war … many English live worse than this.'

> She drift to the window, look quizzical upon the scene, rub her gloved hand on the pane of glass, examine it before saying once more, 'This the way the English live?'
>
> Soon the honourable man inside me was shaking my ribs and thumping my breast, wanting to know, 'Gilbert, what in God's name have you done? You no realise, man? Cha, you married to this woman!'

Andrea Levy, Small Island, *2004, pp20–21, 22*

Commentary on Activity 5

Hortense's point of view is given through a number of methods, beyond the obvious one that it is her first-person narrative. Her imperative way of speaking, giving orders, is contrasted with Gilbert's softly spoken words. The detail of what she sees, especially things that are broken and out of place, suggest, someone seeing something for the first time with a critical eye. The repetition of 'Just this' and the giving way of her legs focus on her shock and surprise.

Whereas repeated words from Hortense show her amazement, when Gilbert reports her repetition he does so with increasing irritation, until we are given, in direct thought, the idea that he is wondering if he should regret his marriage.

As readers we probably do not take sides in this misunderstanding, but we are being offered a third, more indirect point of view to consider – provided, that is, that we pick up the potential meanings on offer. Hortense has supposedly come from a small island, Jamaica, but it is she who is shocked by the squalor she finds in England, when she expected to be impressed. To her, Britain is the small island. One detail in Gilbert's narrative highlights this: when Hortense rubs the window, he does not comment on its significance, and because it is not in her narrative nor does she. But attentive readers will note that she is wearing a glove, a sign of social standing, and after rubbing the dirty window which soils her (white?) glove she repeats her question. The **semiotics** here suggest that how you view a culture depends upon your point of view, and in this novel English readers are being asked to examine the assumptions they make about cultural superiority over others.

What this shows is that while there can be points of view directed through characters, readers too are involved in the process, sometimes finding meanings that the characters themselves do not.

■ Key terms

Semiotics: relates to the meanings of signs. Signs can be visual (a red light on a traffic light means stop) and signs can be verbal (a white glove could signify innocence, for example). Semiotics, then, looks at the significance of connotations.

AQA Examiner's tip

If the text you are writing about has shifting perspectives, try to say what they contribute to the story overall.

🔍 Points of view in poetry

Although poems sometimes give multiple points of view, more frequently they keep to one or two. Poetry tends to condense narratives, which may in part account for this. If only one point of view is given, then there is potential for ambiguity – what would the story be like if it were told by another voice which is not heard? Some of the best examples of re-creative responses to literature look at a text from the point of view of a voice that is absent from the original text. This process does two things:

■ It provides scope for a piece of creative writing.

■ It sheds potentially new light on the original text, perhaps making us less sure of the 'truth' behind the story we have been given.

Activity 6

Read carefully the poem *Sister Maude* below. Then answer the following questions:

1. What would you say is the plot of this poem?
2. How would you describe the poem's point of view?
3. Whose voices are absent in the poem?
4. What might these voices have to say?
5. How does considering question 4 throw new light on the poem?

Sister Maude

Who told my mother of my shame,
Who told my father of my dear?
Oh who but Maude, my sister Maude,
Who lurked to spy and peer.

Cold he lies, as cold as stone,
With his clotted curls about his face:
The comeliest corpse in all the world
And worthy of a queen's embrace.

You might have spared his soul, sister,
Have spared my soul, your own soul too:
Though I had not been born at all,
He'd never have looked at you.

My father may sleep in Paradise,
My mother at Heaven-gate:
But sister Maude shall get no sleep
Either early or late.

My father may wear a golden gown,
My mother a crown may win;
If my dear and I knocked at Heaven-gate
Perhaps they'd let us in:
But sister Maude, oh sister Maude,
Bide you with death and sin.

Christina Rossetti, 1860

Link: extract 12

To complete Activity 7 you will need to use *The Patriot* which is printed in the Extracts section at the back of this book, extract 12.

Link

For a Commentary on Activity 7, see p54.

The Patriot

As with other chapters, this one closes by looking at the poem *The Patriot*, this time focusing on its point of view.

Activity 7

1. How do we know that the narrative in this poem is from the point of view of The Patriot? Are there any places in the poem where the narrative may be from a different perspective?
2. Write (in prose, or poetry if you wish) versions of this story as they might be told by others who are mentioned in this poem.

1 Consider the novels that you are studying. Choose a representative section (say a chapter) and discuss the following issues:

- What is the point of view in this section of the novel? How close or distant is it from the action? Can you find an ideological point of view?

- Does the point of view remain constant or does it shift?

2 Consider the poetry texts that you are studying, and discuss the following issues for various poems:

- What is the point of view in the poem? How close or distant is it from the action? Can you find an ideological point of view?

- Does the title have the same point of view as the rest of the poem?

- Do a re-creative exercise, where you rewrite a poem, or part of the poem, from a different point of view. You can do this in verse or prose. What do you learn about the original in doing this?

■ Commentaries

Commentary on Activity 2

1 You will have given a frame-by-frame account of what you can see.

2 You will almost certainly have connected different frames and begun to develop a sort of plot. You may have written something like:

A man is working at his computer. He gets up to go to the fridge, but on his way to the kitchen is interrupted by a voice upstairs asking him what time it is. By the time he opens the fridge door he has forgotten what he was looking for in the first place.

3 Narrative methods that you may have noticed include: a character is created; there is a sense of place; there is a chronology to the story; there is a plot of sorts; there is speech, some of which is attributed (his) and some of which is not (the voice upstairs); there is thought. There is also the expectation that the reader will fill in the gaps (literal gaps here between the images) to create a continuous plot and narrative.

Commentary on Activity 3

1 We now find out that the voice upstairs belongs to a woman – we might assume she is the man's wife or partner. She is drawing something, which might be a comic strip, but we do not get close enough to see. We find out that it is 1.15 at night, not day. From the look on her face she might have asked about the time because she is bored.

2 The most obvious crucial difference is that this time the story is drawn from her point of view, and given that she is not the main participant, we cannot make up a plot from this in the way we could before. We can only see what she sees, which is not much.

Commentary on Activity 6

1 Some aspects of the plot are clear, others less so. The narrator of the poem has had an illicit affair with a man who has been killed. The narrator blames her sister Maude for informing about the affair, and hints that Maude may have betrayed her sister through sexual jealousy. Among various hints and possibilities brought about by words like 'may' and 'if', the final lines are certain – Maude will go to hell for what she has done.

2   The poem is told entirely from the point of view of the narrator. Some or even all of the poem is spoken directly to Maude, which accounts for the uncertainties the reader faces; while they both know, within their fictional world, the details of what happened and who they are, we as readers are less certain. It is tempting to believe everything you are told by the main narrative voice, as they are in control of the story, but it is possible for narrators to tell only part of the story, and for what they say to be in various ways unreliable.

3   Because we only hear from the (unnamed) narrator, lots of voices are absent, most especially that of Sister Maude, the father/mother, and the dead lover. The implication is that Maude did what she did out of jealousy and spite – but the narrator would say that, wouldn't she?

4   A very different story about duty, morality, family shame, Victorian moral customs, and so on, could be told.

5   Thinking about other ways of telling the story highlights how important it can be to consider point of view. We can never, in one sense, get the 'whole story', only a version – and that can set us thinking about other possible ways of seeing what happens both in life and in stories. Re-creative writing of literary texts can stem from this line of thought.

Commentary on Activity 7

1   Pronouns always tell you a lot about narrative point of view. In this poem the dominant pronouns belong to the first person – 'I' and 'me'. The narrative voice which speaks the poem refers to the people who have rejected him with the pronoun 'they', which puts a distance between him and his opponents. However, when the narrator says, 'And you see my harvest', who is being referred to as 'you'? Is it another person within the fictional story being told, or is it more a sort of 'you as reader'?

There are, though, two places where it can be argued that the narrative is not in the first person – these are the title and the subtitle. We cannot be sure, of course, but if the two titles are narrated by a different source than the rest of the poem, then they contain more potential significance: they indicate what we are meant to think about the story we are about to be told. If, on the other hand, they are narrated by the same voice as the poem, then they are just part of his version of events.

2   Because the narrative of the poem itself is in the first person, Browning is able to create considerable ambiguity by his character hinting at events, without giving them the objective detail that would come with a third-person narrative. These hints and ambiguities will have allowed you to give various other interpretations when you have creatively reconstructed the narrative in question 2.

Summary

In this chapter you have considered aspects of point of view, and seen how words to describe point of view are also used to describe ideological perspectives. This means that thinking about where the story is coming from, whose views are allowed to dominate and whether we accept/approve of these views, is a vital part of the reading process.

Destination

Aims of the chapter:

- Looks at different aspects of narrative in order to consider the narrative as a whole.

- Explains that all parts of the narrative process contribute to the overall effects and meanings of the story being told.

This chapter looks at aspects of narrative in a more holistic way, drawing together the different aspects you have studied in earlier chapters, to consider the narrative as a whole. In the real world our experiences can seem quite random, shapeless, without any overarching point or meaning. In the fictional world of stories, though, there is usually a greater sense of wholeness and completion.

Reading as a journey

As we have worked our way through different ways of looking at aspects of narrative, we have noticed metaphors that often derive from visual sources, such as point of view, perspective, and so on. In this chapter, the metaphor changes to one involving a journey of discovery and exploration. We have explored aspects of narrative in the texts we are studying, and looked at how various methods are used – but where does it get us in the end? What have we ultimately found out about the text? What interpretations can be made from what we have seen? What is our destination?

Put another way, much can be gained and enjoyed from looking at how texts work in terms of their narratives, but if we then stop at that point, it is rather like giving up on a journey before you actually get anywhere important. We need to come to some wider conclusions based on what we have seen in detail along the way. In terms of studying AS-level English Literature you need to consider the following:

- What have I seen about the methods used and how does this help me come to an interpretation?
- Is there contextual material worth considering in helping me come to an interpretation?
- Are different interpretations now possible? Is one more convincing than another?

In other words – and this time using the official language of the Assessment Objectives – having done the exploratory work which has looked in detail at the ways in which form, structure and language shape meanings in literary texts (AO2), you will now broaden your horizons by showing your understanding of the significance and influence of some of the contexts in which literary texts are written and received (AO4) through making connections and comparisons between different literary texts, informed by possible interpretations of other readers (AO3). In order to do this well you will need to write informed and relevant responses to literary texts, using appropriate terminology and concepts, and coherent, accurate written expression (AO1).

Link

See the Introduction to this book for more on the Assessment Objectives.

Bringing all four Assessment Objectives together in this way, you will be illustrating that Unit 1 is a comprehensive unit that covers all the main elements of AS Level study of English literature. You have begun with the analysis of textual detail before moving on to look at wider implications.

Remember

The word 'text' refers to a whole text, which in terms of poetry may be a long single poem or a collection of shorter ones.

Wider implications

What exactly are these wider implications, as suggested by AOs 3 and 4? They can be subdivided into the following categories:

- If you are looking at part of a text, what is its relationship with the whole text? What is its relationship with the other texts being studied? What common ground can be found?
- What is the relationship between the opening of the text and its closure? How do these two vital parts of the text relate to each other?
- Are there relevant ideas that arise out of the writer's life and times which may be helpful when considering the text? These can be called contexts of production.
- Are there relevant ideas that arise out of contemporary ideas and situations which may affect the way the text can be read? These can be called contexts of reception.
- Can different critical methods be applied to the text? What ambiguities and uncertainties arise from studying it? Can these ambiguities be seen positively?

Exam questions

Clearly, how the exam questions are worded will depend in part on the actual texts you are studying; there will be four in total: two novels and two poetry texts. Section A of the exam will focus on single texts, while Section B will ask you to compare texts. The following sample questions show you how the paper is designed: as with all sample questions, try to see beyond the set texts themselves into a broader scheme of enquiry.

In Section A you will write about one set text, so there will be considerable choice available to you.

Link

See the Introduction for more detail on the exam requirements.

Examples of questions from Section A

1. Poetry: Robert Browning, named poems
   a. Write about the ways Browning tells the story of the Pied Piper of Hamelin in Chapter VII (7) of the poem.
   b. *The Pied Piper of Hamelin* is subtitled 'A Child's Story'. Is it simply a child's story?
2. Novel: Khaled Hosseini, *The Kite Runner*
   a. Write about the ways Hosseini opens the story in Chapter 1.
   b. Some readers see the title *The Kite Runner* as representing a journey. What meanings can you find in the title of the text?

In Section B the questions are more general, and although there is some choice, there will be less than in Section A.

Examples of questions from Section B

1 Write about the importance of places in the telling of the stories in three texts that you have studied.

2 Write about some of the ways in which characters have been created in the three texts you have studied.

AQA Examiner's tip

It is always useful to have a working knowledge of what your exam paper will be like. Bear in mind, though, that exam questions are not written to absolute formulae, and that ultimately your job is to answer the question exactly as required.

The Patriot

In a book such as this one it is often necessary to look at parts of texts for illustrative purposes. The longer study of complete texts needs to be done by you in the light of what this book is saying. To consider how the idea of destination works we will use the single poem *The Patriot,* which we have already looked at in previous chapters.

The Patriot
An Old Story

It was roses, roses, all the way,
With myrtle mixed in my path like mad;
The house-roofs seemed to heave and sway,
The church-spires flamed, such flags they had,
A year ago on this very day.

The air broke into a mist with bells,
The old walls rocked with the crowd and cries.
Had I said, 'Good folk, mere noise repels –
But give me your sun from yonder skies!'
They had answered 'And afterward, what else?'

Alack, it was I who leaped at the sun
To give it my loving friends to keep!
Naught man could do, have I left undone:
And you see my harvest, what I reap
This very day, now a year is run.

There's nobody on the house-tops now –
Just a palsied few at the windows set;
For the best of the sight is, all allow,
At the Shambles' Gate – or, better yet,
By the very scaffold's foot, I trow.

I go in the rain, and, more than needs,
A rope cuts both my wrists behind;
And I think, by the feel, my forehead bleeds,
For they fling, whoever has a mind,
Stones at me for my year's misdeeds.

Thus I entered, and thus I go!
In triumphs, people have dropped down dead,
'Paid by the world, what dost thou owe
Me?' – God might question; now instead,
'Tis God shall repay: I am safer so.

Robert Browning

So far we have found out the following by looking at some of the building blocks of narrative.

Setting (places)

There are a few details about the place. It seems to be a walled town or even a city, given that we are told there are 'church-spires' in the plural. The reference to 'house-roofs' might imply a place of some grandeur. Not even the country is specified.

Time and sequence

In terms of actual historical time there are few clues. The subtitle, which could suggest that the story is set in the distant past, is subtly ambiguous. Is this an old story because it is historical, or is it an old story because it is one told many times, with as much reference to now as to any other time?

There is, though, a clear and precise timescale to the action of the poem. The voice narrating the poem compares his public reception a year ago with his reception now. The preciseness of the time here, exactly a year, helps to highlight the difference between then and now.

Is it the narrator who has changed, or the public? Although he says he has committed 'misdeeds', this may be ironic – it could be how the public perceives what he has done.

Characters and characterisation

There is the patriot himself who narrates the poem, and the people of the city. The patriot has a label: he is 'The Patriot', but has no name. The people of the city are described a year ago, when they are enthusiastic about what The Patriot is doing, but now they are absent, waiting offstage somewhere else to see him hanged. Only 'a palsied few' remain in the town itself, presumably because they cannot move.

Voices

The dominant voice is that of The Patriot, who sounds as though he is making a final speech before his execution. The voice is resigned and thoughtful rather than aggressive and angry, which presumably it could be, given his treatment.

There is one other brief piece of reported speech, the collective 'cries' of the people celebrating his return. There are also some short pieces of direct speech that *might have been* spoken. In the first instance he pretends to ask for the impossible and the grateful crowd are willing to give him anything. The second imaginary piece of direct speech involves God, who makes the moral point that earthly riches are nothing compared with eternal ones.

Point of view

In this poem the dominant pronouns belong to the first person – 'I' and 'me'. There are, though, two places where it can be argued that the narrative is not in the first person – these are the title and the subtitle.

Because the narrative of the poem itself is in the first person, Browning is able to create considerable ambiguity by his character hinting at events, without giving them the objective detail that would come with a third-person narrative.

These reminders should help us as we now widen our consideration by looking at aspects of context and interpretation. We will begin by looking at some issues to do with key aspects of the text itself.

Commentary on Activity 1

The main title uses the definite article 'The', whereas the subtitle uses the indefinite article 'An'. This suggests that the poem is about someone specific (*the* patriot) on the one hand and yet tells one of a number of stories (*an* old story) on the other.

The word 'patriot' derives originally from the Greek word *patrios*, meaning 'of one's father'. A patriot, then, loves the fatherland, but for many readers, certainly within British culture, to be a patriot is not necessarily a good thing. Dr Johnson famously wrote that 'Patriotism is the last refuge of a scoundrel'. There is a long tradition in British culture of the word being used to suggest either foolishness or cunning – as bald a title as *The Patriot* hints that this poem is not going to end happily.

As we have already seen when considering aspects of time in the poem, 'An old story' can be read in different ways. The phrase could refer to the fact that this is a poem set in past times, or it could suggest that its an old story because it is telling the same old story – in other words, there have been many such stories and they all turn out the same.

Commentary on Activity 2

What we find out

> A year ago he was a hero.
> He received a rapturous reception.
> He tried to help his friends.
> He is now going to the scaffold.
> Only a few watch now.

What we are not told

> What he had done to be so popular.
> Where the action is set.
> In what time the action is set.
> What he has done in the intervening year.
> Why he is being executed.

In many ways what we are not told makes the more interesting list. By being so inexact about many of the core things that make up the narrative, Browning is deliberately making us look beyond the specifics of a story and inviting us to consider wider significances.

So one possible reading is that the patriot in this poem is presented as both wise and foolish. When describing the entry to the city, he provides an imaginary conversation with the crowd ('Had I said'). He knows that if he had asked for the sun, they would have offered it and more – and yet it would have been an impossible thing to ask for. He knows that the crowd is fickle, and will promise anything because they are swept up in the occasion in a way that he was not. And yet for 'my loving friends', friends whom he knows will be disloyal, he 'leaped at the sun' and ruined everything.

Even as he walks to the scaffold he is detached enough to know where the best views of hanging are. His line 'Thus I entered and thus I go' is resigned rather than bitter, the resignation stressed by the way Browning uses repetition in both vocabulary and syntax.

He is presented, then, as someone who now knows the world and the people in it.

Activity 1

This poem has both a title, *The Patriot*, and a subtitle, 'An Old Story'. Both these phrases carry possible cultural associations; in other words, when you read them, you may be aware that they have various possible meanings, both for you and for others.

Working in a group if possible, and using reference works such as a dictionary and a dictionary of quotations, make a list of your initial responses to these titles.

Did you know?

Dr (Samuel) Johnson (1709–84) wrote the first standard dictionary of the English language, which took him eight years to complete and was first published in 1755.

Activity 2

Make a list of what Browning allows you to find out about the actions of the narrator of the poem and then make a list of what you do not know – and which, if you did, would make the poem more straightforward in its meaning.

Activity 3

Look at the final verse of the poem. What sort of conclusion does it give to the poem? Compare this ending to way that the poem begins.

Commentary on Activity 3

The opening line of the poem 'It was roses, roses all the way' is exceptionally rhythmic, with its uncomplicated vocabulary and its repetition. By the end of the poem, though, things are a good deal more complicated. The verse begins with two end-stopped lines, 'Thus I entered and thus I go!' followed by, 'In triumphs, people have dropped down dead'. Both lines carry the suggestion of someone resigned to his fate, aware that triumph and death are always close. The last three lines, however, are much more enigmatic, and the verse form emphasises this, with its more fractured use of lines.

There is a sustained metaphor of paying, owing, repaying which runs through the last three lines, but its precise meaning seems elusive. If the patriot is 'safer', safer than what? Safer in the hands of God than men?

▓ Contexts of production

While all texts have to be read within a contextual framework – there can be no such thing as a text existing in a world of its own – how much context you apply to your answers, and what sort of context, involves making careful, thoughtful choices. This poem does not appear to have any connection to Browning's own personal experience, for example, so there is no real point in going into authorial biography to help us.

However, there are some more **literary contexts** to do with the time of writing which might help when considering the poem as a whole.

Dramatic monologues

Browning is renowned for his writing of dramatic monologues. Dramatic monologues are narrated by a single voice, often of a central character in a story. As we have already seen, though, first-person narratives are subjective, so the reader has to work out that there is more to the story than the speaking voice knows or is willing to acknowledge.

This information is useful for us here up to a point, in that as readers we certainly have to work hard to find meanings because so much vital information is missing. It would be hard, though, to say that this poem is 'dramatic', because the narrator does not appear to be talking to anyone else within the world of the poem.

🔍 Victorian poetry

Victorian poetry is sometimes seen as rather sentimental, milking emotion out of stories of lost love and medieval romance. There is certainly a medieval feel to the setting of this poem, albeit in general terms. So here we have two historical strands: a Victorian text, with its contexts of Victorian times, is itself representing an even earlier age.

On the other hand, the poem is marked by surprisingly little emotion – the narrator seems to be completely resigned to his fate, and although there are expressions of regret they are not sentimentally overemphasised.

So what we can see here is that contexts of production need to be evaluated carefully and always measured against the core text itself. For our purposes, both here and in an exam, we are concerned with this poem, not with other poems by Browning or indeed other poems written when Browning was alive.

Contexts of reception

It was noted above that there were two historical strands when looking at contexts of production. But if we now consider contexts of reception there is another obvious question to ask: Why are we studying a poem written nearly 150 years ago? Is it just interesting as an old text, or are we studying it because it says something to us now, because in a sense it has outgrown its original contexts and can now be seen to work within new contextual frameworks? Or put another way, although we considered that the text could be looked at through thinking about contexts at the time of production, surely what has happened after the text was written, and indeed what is happening now, also need to be considered?

When talking about historical contexts, especially with texts that are 'old', there is an inevitable, and not always very helpful, tendency to generalise: to say that all Elizabethans were racist/sexist/ homophobic and so on, is not very helpful and not true. When looking at contemporary contexts, in the circumstances that affect our readings in the here and now, we can be much more specific about the contexts we are applying and much more receptive to views other than our own.

The 20th century and the first years of the 21st have seen warfare, sometimes on a mass scale, with millions involved in worldwide conflict, and sometimes on a smaller scale, yet still with horror and suffering. Whether it be to recruit new forces to replace the dead, or to keep public opinion in favour of a war that on television looks awful, countries and their politicians have needed to ensure that there is public support for war. One way in which they have done this is to invoke notions of patriotism: our country is right and good, the enemy is wrong and evil.

We are all familiar with images of mass propaganda and recruitment from World War One, for example. In more recent times there have been wars that have been highly controversial, with many objectors claiming they should not be fought at all. In these

Fig. 1 *A recruitment poster from World War One*

wars in particular, when public opinion is much more divided, notions of patriotism are invoked both by those who support the cause and by those who deny it.

The problem with notions of rightness and goodness, wrong and evil, is that they are shifting terms. What happens when the war is over, when forms of peace are made? What do we do with those who fought for the ex-cause and who survived, but who are maybe injured or embarrassing to have around for various reasons?

Evidence would suggest that those whom the Americans call 'vets' (veterans) are not always welcome back. They find it difficult to settle, they behave in unorthodox ways, they have lived through incredible stress. Is that what this poem is about – the universally fickle way in which societies treat their heroes?

 Activity 4

Now considering the poem overall, and the contextual material presented above, what ideas would you say are most important in the poem *The Patriot*? What in the end is the poem saying? Why should we still read it now?

Commentary on Activity 4

What we are ideally doing in answering this question is incorporating our work on narrative with a sense of wider context. We have noticed much that is absent here that we might expect to find in a story: details of time and place, motivation of character, and so on. This, while not necessarily appealing to everyone, can be justified by showing that in deliberately not being specific, Browning is being universal. He is talking about a number of issues which seem to have universal meanings. These could include:

▓ the briefness of success and popularity

▓ the manipulation of mass groups

▓ the fickle ways in which heroes are first loved and then ignored

▓ that with celebrity can come excess

▓ that patriotism is a shifting concept

▓ that heroes become villains when the cause is finished.

To me the last bullet point resonates most. It is possible in the same American city, for example, to see heroic receptions for soldiers returning from Iraq and street beggars who fought in Vietnam. What Browning is saying, it seems to me, is that there will be times when your country needs you, followed by times when it does not.

You may notice in the paragraph above that the most favoured issue has been given as a personal preference. There often comes a point in weighing up different interpretations when you want to give your own preferred reading, while acknowledging that there are others. At this point in your answer it is fully acceptable to refer to yourself as 'I/me'.

Conclusion

The word 'narrative' has its origins in the Greek word for knowledge. Ultimately, then, looking at narrative involves looking at knowledge. Put this another way and you can ask yourself the following questions, taking the idea of 'knowing' here in its broadest sense. For any text, at any point in the text, you can ask:

▓ Who knows what?

▓ When do/did they know it?

▓ How do they know it?

But there is one further point to make here. Because this is literature, and so representational, we are not dealing with the real world, we are dealing with a fictional world designed for readers. So now we can slightly reconfigure the questions above and also ask of any text at any point:

▓ What does the reader know?

▓ When does/did the reader find this out?

▓ How did they find it out?

Bear these questions in mind and they will prove invaluable as you tackle questions in the exam.

8 Preparing for the exam

Aim of the chapter:

■ Enables you to be well prepared for your exam.

Always make sure that your **preparation and revision** involve a specific task, with a specific amount of time allocated and a clear end result. **Revision** involves looking over something you have done already, which is important, but it is equally important to do something new, to prepare some thoughts and ideas on topics that have not been covered so far.

■ Link

See the Introduction to this book for an outline of the exam requirements.

Always make sure that your focused stint of work leaves you **better informed** about the key topic – in this case narrative – than you were before you started. Also make sure that you have a **written record** of what you have prepared so that you can glance over it in the final few days before the exam.

This short final chapter gives you some hints on final preparation for your AS-level English Literature exam – some of which apply to all your exams, whatever the subject. These hints are based on the assumption that you have worked hard up to this point and that you have read the texts and know them well.

■ Using this book

One obvious way of preparing for the exam is to use this book. Take each chapter in turn and apply its focus to the actual set texts you are studying.

You might also, along with your teacher, think of some ways of focusing more specifically on some of the four texts you have studied for this unit. Here are some points to consider, bearing in mind that this is an open-book exam:

■ This unit is organised under the title 'Aspects of Narrative'. This means that you do not need to know everything there is to know about these texts: your starting point for revision will be ideas about narrative.

■ Remember that in Section A of the exam you will be required to write in some detail on one of the four texts. Which text will it be? How many of the four do you intend to prepare for in this way?

■ Remember that in Section B you will need to write in a much more general way about the three other texts you have studied (that is, not including the one you have used in Section A). Do you have a good overview of them, and can you find significant parts of them without delay?

■ What use do you expect to make of the open-book facility? Section A will ask you to look at a specific section of a text, but you will not necessarily have time to read it all. How well do you know your text so that a skim reading will suffice?

↰ Short answers

Both parts of Section A involve short answers – you will have about half an hour for each. Short answers differ from essays in that you do not need to provide introductions and conclusions. You simply get on and answer the question directly.

You will need to practise this sort of writing.

↰ The essay

In Section B you will be writing an essay on an aspect of narrative across three texts. What in outline will this involve?

■ You will need to write a short introduction giving an overview of the topic as it affects your chosen texts.

■ You will need to check carefully whether the question asks you to 'compare' your texts or just to 'write about' them. If asked to compare, you will need to ensure that you do some cross-referencing of the texts – but you do not have to keep doing this all the time. If asked to write about the topic, you do not need to compare texts, but you might occasionally choose to do so.

AQA Examiner's tip

At some points in your preparation programme, actually write some sample answers and show them to your teacher for feedback and guidance.

- You will need to provide some evidence from each of the three texts, but with limited time you cannot be expected to say everything.
- You will need to write approximately the same amount on each text, but there is no rule that says they have to be exactly equal.
- You will need to tie your ideas together at the end with a brief conclusion.

You will need to practise this sort of writing.

Learning to quote and refer

How are you going to prepare for giving textual evidence? One form of evidence is direct quotation – you are far more likely to use this with the poetry than the prose fiction.

Quotation can involve quoting chunks of text, but it can also involve integrating words or phrases into your own syntax. So while you could quote from *The Patriot* by writing:

> Browning begins his poem with his narrator describing past glories:
> 'It was roses, roses, all the way,
> With myrtle mixed in my path like mad'

You could also write:

> In his opening lines Browning's references to 'roses' and 'myrtle' placed in the patriot's 'path like mad' help to create an initial mood of celebration.

The second method is often better as it lets you get on with your argument while at the same time showing that you know the text well. Practise this method of quoting and you will soon find that you become adept at it.

Equally effective, though, can be **reference**, especially when you are writing about a novel. Reference is when you show awareness of an event, a character, a place, and so on, by referring to it with knowledge rather than using the exact words the author uses. Keeping for the moment to the lines above, if you refer to them you would write something like:

> Browning's references to flowers being thrown in the path of the patriot give an immediate sense of celebration.

To summarise, here is a list of points to bear in mind when you are using quotation and reference:

- You should support your arguments with frequent and relevant textual evidence.
- Quotations should be brief.
- Quotations should be accurate.
- The best quotations are embedded in your own sentences.
- Reference to the text can also help to give evidence: close references can often work better than quotation.
- Quotations and references should never stand alone: they should be used in support of specific points you are making.

So how much learning do you need to do for an open-book exam? Probably more than you might imagine. If you have to stop at every point to check even the smallest detail then you will lose momentum and continuity. In the end you need to be able to refer to the texts with appropriate detail depending on the question. Only practice in answering such questions will show you how much you really need.

💡 The exam itself

It is common among students to talk of dreading exams, but this can sometimes be overplayed. Exams are a fact of the system we are all in, so we might as well make the most of them.

If you are well prepared then exams should be seen, in part anyway, as a chance to show what you know. And the nature of English literature as a subject also means you should find some space in your head to think in the exam itself.

It is never really appropriate to say 'good luck' to someone before an exam, because exams are not about luck. They are about being well prepared in advance, and thoughtful on the day itself.

Hint

As a general rule, short concentrated bursts of work followed by periods of relaxation are much better than long stretches of time which deliver little in terms of end product.

AQA Examiner's tip

The very highest marks usually go to students who give the impression that they are thinking about the topic rather than repeating what they have said before. Amongst all the pressure of the event itself, try to find time to think clearly and say exactly what you want to.

2 Dramatic Genres: Aspects of Tragedy
Introduction to Unit 2

Aims of the chapter:

■ Introduces Unit 2, dramatic genres: aspects of tragedy.

■ Considers some general ideas about the study of your coursework texts.

■ Specifies what you need to submit for your coursework.

Tragedy is a complex form of theatre, and in this unit you will explore several aspects of tragedy which will lead into your coursework. The specification asks for the compulsory study of at least one Shakespeare play, so it should come as no surprise that the works of William Shakespeare are seen as central to our understanding of tragedy. In addition to your Shakespeare play you will also study another play which falls into the tragic genre. The range of plays that could be chosen for this non-Shakespeare study is wide and varied, with many time periods and sub-genres of plays available, but the play you will study will ordinarily be chosen for you by your teacher. Because the range of plays is so wide, it is important that you don't skip activities in this book on texts you aren't studying, since all the activities will help you develop understanding and skills that you can apply to your own coursework texts.

■ Reading and studying plays

Drama: a difficult genre

When dealing with plays, you should remember that the text your are reading was not written to be read, but to be performed. Much can be learned by reading the words on the page, but that is not the entire text. Drama texts consist not only of language, but also visual aspects, including set, movement and sound. Whilst English Literature focuses on the written text, you should be aware of these other aspects and of the different interpretations of the text that these can give. For example, the same words might be spoken by an actor using different facial expressions to give a different meaning, or the atmosphere of a play might be altered significantly by the amount of light on the stage. Your job is not to discuss the effect of these aspects, but to be aware of the different interpretations they could create.

💡 Active reading

As with Unit 1, it is important that you read each text at least once to get the overview of the plot. When you have chosen a title for your coursework, you will find it beneficial to read your text through again, focussing specifically on the theme and/or question you have chosen. As you go along, make notes of key moments, quotations and points you could use in your essay. Since you will be able to use your notes when writing your coursework, these notes will form the basis of your plans. It will be much easier to spot important quotations when you are reading through your text than to search through the whole text looking for something relevant.

Tragedy is a complex form of theatre, and in this unit you will explore several aspects of tragedy that will lead into your coursework. The specification asks for the compulsory study of at least one Shakespeare play, so it should come as no surprise that the works of William Shakespeare are seen as central to our understanding of tragedy.

Assessment of Unit 2

This unit will be assessed by the production of a coursework portfolio of two pieces of work:

1 A study of an aspect of the tragic genre with regard to a Shakespeare play (1,200–1,500 words).

2 A study of an aspect of the tragic genre with regard to another play (1,200–1,500 words).

One of the two pieces can be in the form of a creative (or more accurately **re-creative**) exercise – we will look in more detail at this creative writing in Chapter 16. At the end of each of Chapters 9–15 we offer you and your teacher some suggestions for coursework tasks, related to what you have studied in the chapter.

9 Introducing tragedy

Aims of the chapter:

- Introduces tragedy as a literary genre.

- Considers a range of examples of other forms of tragedy.

- Sets out the differences between literary tragedy and popular, everyday forms of tragedy.

💡 Key terms

Classical: usually refers to plays written in ancient Greece or Rome.

Epic: refers to a play that has a grand or ambitious theme.

Modern: most often refers to plays written in the late 19th or 20th century.

Domestic: refers to drama set in a household. It does not have a grand or ambitious theme.

Contemporary: refers to plays written in the late 20th or 21st century.

Disorder: inversion of the normal order in a society.

▨ Assessment of Unit 2

This unit will be assessed by the production of a coursework portfolio of two pieces of work.

1 A study of an aspect of the tragic genre with regard to a Shakespeare play (1200–1500 words).

2 A study of an aspect of the tragic genre with regard to another play (1200–1500 words).

One of the two pieces can be in the form of a creative (or more accurately re-creative) exercise – we will look in more detail at this creative writing in Chapter 16. At the end of each of Chapters 9–15 we offer you and your tutor some suggestions for coursework tasks, related to what you have studied in the chapter.

▨ What is tragedy?

Tragedy is a genre (or type) of drama that ends with the death of the main character. In principle, there are two main kinds of tragedy. The first kind is the form written initially by classical Greek dramatists, such as Sophocles, Aeschylus and Euripedes, and later refined by Shakespeare and his contemporaries, in which the audience witnesses terrible chaos and breakdown in a society. We may usefully label this kind of tragedy as **classical** or **epic** tragedy.

The second type of tragedy is usually known as **modern** or **domestic** tragedy. It may initially seem less ambitious than classical or epic tragedy, but confronts many of the same issues. It usually involves the breakdown of a family, showing the corruption and chaos that lurks beneath the surface of apparent domestic order. This type of tragedy was established in the 19th century by writers such as Henrik Ibsen and August Strindberg, and was later refined by playwrights such as Eugene O'Neill and Arthur Miller.

Many **contemporary** writers have been influenced by both of these traditions. For example, Tony Harrison is a poet and dramatist who is much influenced by classical Greek tragedy, while Timberlake Wertenbaker has drawn upon epic and modern ideas of tragedy for her plays. Tragedy would seem to be a form of theatre that still appeals today after thousands of years of development.

Tragedies offer a bleak vision of life since they concentrate on failure, conflict and disaster. In most dramas of this type, three aspects are emphasised: **suffering**, **chaos** and **death**.

- **Suffering** is what the characters must endure in a tragedy. The audience watches how the suffering is created and how the central characters deal with their suffering.

- **Chaos** (which we might also term **disorder**) can be both personal and social. In some tragedies the central character breaks down; in others the whole of society disintegrates, while in several both the characters and the society fall apart and collapse. Chaos usually leads to death.

- At the end of the drama the cast and the audience are left staring at the reality of **death** and its consequences.

In this way, tragedies are very ambitious plays because they carry huge subject matter and themes. They deal in matters of life and death, and for this reason alone may be considered an important literary form.

Some examples of tragedies

Plays

You and your partner have probably developed a long list of texts that involve aspects of tragedy. You may have instantly thought of plays that you have read or heard of before, especially the tragedies by William Shakespeare, such as *Macbeth*, *Hamlet* and *King Lear*. You may also have heard of a few modern tragedies, such as *Hedda Gabler* and *Death of a Salesman*.

Television programmes and computer games

Most likely, though, you will have thought of texts that often end in the death of the main character or characters. Television soap operas such as *Coronation Street* and *EastEnders* very often incorporate elements of tragic drama in their storylines, as do crime investigation shows like *Waking the Dead* and *CSI: Miami*. Computer games such as *Doom* and *Resident Evil* also have sophisticated tragic plot.

Films

Film is a particularly rich area to consider since many plots use motifs and ideas loosely from the tragic genre. *Titanic* (1997) is a romantic drama, directed by James Cameron, about the sinking of the RMS *Titanic* on its ill-fated voyage in 1912. Essentially, the film is a love story between Rose DeWitt Bukater (played by Kate Winslett) and Jack Dawson (played by Leonardo DiCaprio), which ends in tragedy when, after the sinking, Rose realises that Jack has frozen to death and has to release him into the sea. There is a personal tragedy to their story, but also a wider tragedy about other people on board the stricken liner. It is shown that even the most sophisticated aspects of human culture (such as a massive liner) can eventually fall into ruin.

Fig. 1 *Rose and Jack struggling to survive in* Titanic *(1997)*

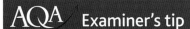

Fig. 2 *Sméagol (Gollum) from Peter Jackson's adaption of Lord of the Rings*

Redemption: making up for one's faults, or being saved from the consequences of one's earlier actions. Usually, however, this does not happen in tragedies – the character fails to be redeemed.

Tristan & Isolde (2006) is another film that incorporates some elements of the tragic genre. Set in post-Roman Cornwall and Ireland, the story tells the ill-fated love triangle of Tristan, King Mark and Isolde. Tristan is torn between his love for Isolde and his loyalty to Mark, a man whom he has loved as his father. The couple eventually begin an affair behind Mark's back, which is later discovered, and culminates in Tristan's death. The story of Tristan and Isolde is ancient, probably first written down in the middle of the 12th century, but it has inspired many retellings.

With both these narratives there is a link between powerful love and the sadness of having that love end in tragedy. Probably the most famous story of this type is *Romeo and Juliet*, which was written by Shakespeare in 1595, and given a contemporary makeover in the 1997 film version, directed by Baz Luhrmann and set in a hip, modern suburb of Verona. The story of the two 'star-crossed lovers' is a common plot within the tragic genre, and it is one you will witness again and again.

In this sense, you can see that tragedies are timeless stories which are still popular now. This may account for why the tragic components of film trilogies are very popular; for example the fall (though also eventual **redemption**) of Anakin Skywalker in *Star Wars: Episodes I–VI*, and several characters – such as Sméagol (Gollum), Arwen and Boromir – featured in Peter Jackson's adaptation of J.R.R. Tolkien's *Lord of the Rings*. Although the stories of such characters do not always end in death, they do have tragic components.

Real-life events

You may also have thought of many powerful real-life stories that have ended in tragedy, for example the destruction of the World Trade Center on 11 September 2001; the destruction of the *Challenger* Space Shuttle; the early deaths of the rock stars Freddie Mercury and Kurt Cobain; or the untimely death of Princess Diana. Sometimes whole events are labelled 'tragedies', such as the war in Iraq, or the Indian Ocean tsunami. Such real-life events often formed the starting point for stage tragedies written in the past.

Defining the term 'tragedy'

As in some of the examples above, we sometimes use the term 'tragedy' quite loosely. You may have heard your friends say something along the lines of 'It was tragic!' that their favourite football team had been relegated at the end of the season. Listen to the way that television commentators talk about football, especially when teams lose in Cup Finals or major international tournaments. The word 'tragic' is used a lot, but obviously no one has actually died. Tragic is used here to explain events not going in the way a particular person wants them to, and perhaps to emphasise the dramatic qualities of a sporting occasion.

Although we have gained a sense of what tragedy is about – especially in everyday life and culture – we need to define the term more closely, especially when we consider the literary genre of tragedy. In essence, the relegation of a football team is not really a tragedy, and to describe it as such is a misuse of the word. Literary tragedies tend to look at 'bigger' tragic events.

 **Activity 2**

In Unit 1 of this book we looked at the story 'He died a hero' from *Woman's Own* magazine in order to investigate narrative. With a partner, turn back to Chapter 1 (p6) and reread the story there, then read what happens next (opposite). Although we initially discussed the story in terms of an example of narrative, we can now reconsider it as a form of tragedy. When you reread the story, consider the following questions:

- Why do events end in disaster?
- Who is the tragic hero and how does he 'fall'?
- Is there a sense of inevitability about the death?
- Why is there a sense of waste?
- How does the reader feel at the end of the story?

'He died a hero'

It was meant to be a relaxing family holiday by the seaside, but then tragedy struck...

The first Patricia knew of a problem was when her son's friend, Josh, returned to the caravan in a panic.

'He kept saying that Steve was unconscious. It only took a few minutes to run to the beach, but it felt like an eternity.

'The first people I saw were Mark and Laura, who were both crying. I grabbed them in my arms, and then I spotted a crowd of people trying to resuscitate a body lying motionless on the shore. I knew straightaway that it was Steve.'

Tears running down her cheeks and with every step sinking into the soft sand, Patricia couldn't reach her husband fast enough.

'I've some basic first-aid training and took over the mouth-to-mouth procedure from one of the men,' she says. 'I pleaded with Steve to wake up and tried with all my might to revive him until a paramedic got there.'

When an air ambulance arrived to take Steve to Boston Hospital, Patricia was devastated to learn that there wasn't room for her or the children.

'I begged the paramedics to let us go with Steve. But they said that Mark and Laura were in shock and needed medical attention and that a second helicopter was on its way. But it would be taking us to a different hospital.'

'It was like a bad dream. I wanted to be with Steve to tell him I loved him, but I knew the kids needed me too.'

In the middle of all the panic, Patricia phoned her eldest son, James, 20, who was at home in Sheffield and promised to call back the minute she knew more.

As the children were checked over at Grimsby Hospital, Patricia waited patiently for news of Steven. But then came the devastating blow.

'We'd just found out Mark and Laura were OK when a doctor took me to one side,' says Patricia.

'He said, "I'm sorry... They did everything they could to revive him." It was unbearable. I just couldn't take it in.'

> Transport was arranged to take Patricia, Mark and Laura to Boston Hospital, and James met his family there.
>
> 'We were taken into a room where Steve's body was lying on a bed. I took hold of his hand, stroked his hair and broke down. I couldn't believe I'd been robbed of the man I'd loved for 24 years,' says Patricia.
>
> 'He'd always been the life and soul of everything, and then suddenly he was gone.'

🔍 *Commentary on Activity 2*

The story has some of the hallmarks of a literary tragedy and the dialogue of the story could even be part of the text of a play. Events end in disaster because Steven, the tragic hero, is pulled under and does not resurface. He becomes a **noble** hero (putting others' fate above his own) because he is engaged in the rescue of a girl. Steve 'falls' because he tries to complete an almost superhuman feat, and is perhaps too ambitious (a fatal flaw) in the rescue. We learn that he is 'concerned for everyone's safety', making him a responsible and caring man. However, the language of the rest of the article sets up events for a fall. Phrases such as 'happily relaxing', 'teatime' and 'keen to get down to the beach' work as **signifiers** that the given happy circumstances will somehow later fail.

The way the story is written conveys a sense of **inevitability** about the death. We obviously gain this from the headline to the article, but also from the emotive language used by Steven's widow to recount events on that day ('trying to revive her husband' and 'voice strained with emotion'). The fact that Patricia and her children are not allowed to ride in the same helicopter seems only to heighten the sense of tragedy. The moment of death comes some time later in the story, but we can tell that it will happen. We feel an enormous sense of waste, because Steven and his family were very happy and had much to live for. At the same time, the deep love between Steven and Patricia is also celebrated.

At the end of the story, you as the reader could feel several things:

- You might be amazed that such a single moment can rob someone of their life – especially when that person was committing a noble deed. At this point, you probably feel sympathy with Steven's widow.
- You might feel that you have learnt something important from the story – that perhaps the risk Steven took was not worth it – and that if such a moment occurred in your own life you would do well to think about your actions very carefully.
- In seeing a nobler side of human life and activity, you might feel better for having read the story. Again, you have learnt something from it.
- Finally, because the story leads you through something that you know happens in the world, you come to a greater understanding of the world and of other people.

Language such as 'tragedy struck' and 'it was like a bad dream' emphasises how suddenly events can change, and how people's lives can be altered. Although this is a modern story and involves 'real' people, it is quite similar to some of the subject matter looked at by writers of both epic and domestic tragedy. As you will see, the story also has many of the components which form the genre of tragedy, and which we might expect to see in this type of drama.

💡 Key terms

Noble: describes someone who possesses excellent qualities of mind and character and who is not mean or petty.

Signifiers: signs or symbols used in dramatic texts as pointers to the direction of the drama and its meanings.

Inevitability: refers to events that cannot be prevented. They are certain to happen.

Tragedy in literature

While the examples we have looked at above incorporate tragic elements, we have still used the term 'tragedy' very loosely. Tragedy is a specific genre of literature, which operates within a set of **conventions**. As you will have gathered by now, tragedy is one of the oldest literary traditions that exist in the world, although over time the conventions have helped define what needs to happen on stage, and why writers construct tragedies in certain ways. One of the things the audience should feel when watching a tragedy is that somehow the world is a worse place when the tragic hero is no longer part of it.

As we continue through this unit, keep in mind popular and everyday ideas of tragedy, but try to compare them with the literary genre of tragedy. You will need to examine these conventions within your coursework, and comment upon their use in the dramas you study.

Ideas for coursework tasks

In each of Chapters 9–15 we offer you and your teacher some suggestions for coursework tasks, related to what you have studied in the chapter. These are broad suggestions and the exact wording of your task will need to be negotiated with your teacher.

Essay

To what extent does the Shakespearean tragedy you have studied offer a sense of redemption at the end?

Re-creative response

Write a version for a popular magazine of events at the end of the play you are studying. Make sure that your writing gives a clear indication of how readers of your story are meant to respond to events.

In your commentary say why you chose this reading of the play's final scene, and other readings which could have been possible.

Summary

This first chapter in Unit 2 has introduced you to tragedy as a literary genre, to some of the range of forms it can take and to some of the conventions it involves. You have considered examples of tragedy in other fields, such as television programmes and films. You have noted the tragic elements in a contemporary magazine article, and seen how similar elements are incorporated into literary tragedies. Your understanding of the conventions of literary tragedies, and how they compare with popular and everyday ideas of tragedy, will underpin your coursework on the dramas you study.

Key terms

Conventions: the accepted rules, structures and customs we expect to see in a specific genre of writing.

Further reading

Extension (this reading may be a little challenging)

Beroul: The Romance of Tristan, translated by Alan S. Frederick (1970). This is the original 'dark-age' story of the tragedy of Tristan.

The Elizabethan World Picture by E.M.W. Tillyard (1943). This book explains how Elizabethan people imagined the world be be ordered. Shakespeare tragedies normally involve a breakdown of that order.

10   Tragic heroes, villains and victims

AQA Examiner's tip

Your teacher will guide you as to which tragedies you will be reading for your coursework, but because tragedy is probably a new genre for you to study, you may find it useful to look at *Othello* because it is a useful example of how a tragedy works.

 Key terms

Predictive: allowing the audience to predict what will happen to the characters. Writers do this by inserting **signifiers**, or pointers, into the text to 'set up' the circumstances of a drama.

The way that 'tragedy can strike' as 'a bad dream' (as in the story that we looked at in Chapter 9) can be seen in one of Shakespeare's most famous tragedies, *The Tragedy of Othello: The Moor of Venice*, which was written between 1602 and 1604. *Othello* has many of the characteristics of a typical Shakespearean tragedy – and notice the full title, which would have immediately signalled to the Elizabethan audience first watching the drama that it would be about the death of a great or noble person. We concentrate on this play in our exploration of the theme of tragic heroes, victims and villains in this chapter.

A tragic hero: Othello

In the title of this play Othello is described as a Moor. The Moors were Muslim inhabitants of northern Africa, mainly in Algeria and Morocco. Othello would therefore not have been born a Christian, in contrast to most other Shakespearean heroes. Moors were black-skinned, and by using Othello as a tragic hero, Shakespeare was doing something original. Notice too that in contrast to some of the other tragedies we have mentioned, this is an ambitious and epic story. Try to spot similarities and differences with *Othello* in one of the plays you are studying.

In the play, Othello (the tragic hero) descends into chaos or disorder when he is misled by his friend and Lieutenant Iago (the villain) into believing that his wife Desdemona (the victim) is unfaithful. Iago is manipulating Othello because he is jealous and believes that he had been passed over for promotion in favour of Cassio, another lieutenant. At one point in the play Othello actually uses the word 'chaos', though in a loving tone. Desdemona has just left the stage and he almost jokingly says:

> I do love thee, and when I love thee not
> Chaos is come again.

3.3.91–2

The language here is **predictive** of their fate, and these words have a grim irony later on in the drama. After being misled by Iago, Othello becomes a psychological wreck who is filled with rage, doubt and fear. His nobility then gives way to the chaos of desiring revenge on those who have hurt him. Tragedy strikes Othello from 'nowhere' and when he finds out about the affair, it is like a 'bad dream'.

The opening scenes of *Othello* contain a wide diversity of language, ranging from formal speech to conversational everyday language. You might expect Othello's opening lines to say much about his character. The linked extract has him engaging in dialogue with Iago, with Cassio (another lieutenant, whom Othello later suspects of adultery with his wife) over the conflict with the Turks, and with Brabantio (Desdemona's father) over Othello's apparent 'snatching' of his daughter. You may find it easier to understand the text if you read it aloud several times. Your class could also attempt to perform this extract.

Activity 1

Answer the following questions on the linked extract.

1. What does Shakespeare show us about Othello's interactions with other characters in this extract?

2. What different impressions of Othello do you gain from the speeches of the characters around him?

3. What impression do you gain of Othello from the lines 'Let him do his spite...' to '...what lights come yond!' (lines 17–28)?

4. What kind of character does Iago appear to be at this point?

Extension tasks

1. The critic Helen Gardner wrote an essay about Othello in which she describes him as the 'noble Moor', although she also comments that the play is about the 'progressive revelation of the inadequacy of the hero's nobility'. To what extent might this extract support this claim?

2. From this extract, what can the audience infer about the various characters' attitudes towards race and identity?

Link: Extract 1

To complete Activity 1 you will need to use Othello 1.2.1–99 which is printed in the Extract section at the back of this book, extract 1.

Further reading

For a Commentary on Activity 1, see the end of this chapter (p81).

Did you know?

William Shakespeare lived between 1564 and 1616. His birthday is believed to be 23 April, which was also the date of his death. The main period of his interest in tragedy was between 1599 and 1609. The First Folio, the first collected edition of his plays, was printed in 1623.

🔍 A tragic villain: Iago

In the above section, you will have started to see how the character Iago operates. Recognising that he has some considerable power and influence over Othello, it is Iago who manipulates information and events, so that Othello will believe anything he says. In the remainder of the play we see that Iago is a recognisable type of tragic villain, who tries to cause disorder and catastrophe for his own ends. Before, he had lied, telling Brabantio that Othello has bewitched his daughter. Later, he tells Roderigo that Cassio is a drunk, and tells Othello that Desdemona gave Cassio her handkerchief as a **symbol** of her love for him. Shakespeare labels Iago 'honest' to heighten the deception that is occurring, while Iago himself often speaks to the audience in **soliloquies** or **asides** in which they learn of his possible objectives.

Key terms

Symbol: something that stands for something else. In literary texts, the connection is usually not directly stated and the reader is expected to recognise the symbol for what it represents. Symbols are often used in tragedies.

Soliloquy: a speech spoken by a character, who is usually alone on the stage, in which they tell or confess their thoughts to the audience. Soliloquies are often used in tragedies because they tell us about why particular characters are doing something. In films, the technique of voice-over is used to similar effect, to convey the thoughts inside a character's mind.

Aside: a very brief soliloquy within a normal sequence of dialogue, in which a character speaks a short line specifically to the audience, telling their true thoughts about events on stage.

■ Link: extract 2

To complete Activity 2 you will need to use Othello 4.1.1-48, which is printed in the Extracts section at the back of this book, extract 2.

■ Key terms

Verse: rhymed or (most usually) unrhymed poetry that is found in Shakespearean and other drama of the period, and is usually spoken by higher-class or noble characters. The unrhymed form is written in **iambic pentameters** (ten-syllable lines with five stresses) and when performed closely imitates the rhythm of speech in English. It is sometimes called **blank verse**.

Prose: 'normal' speech in paragraphs not poetry. It is usually spoken by lower-class characters or in tragedy when noble characters are caught in a downward spiral.

■ Further reading

For a Commentary on Activity 2, see the end of this chapter (p82).

■ Activity 2

In the linked extract, Iago's manipulation is beginning to take effect. Discuss Othello's and Iago's language at this point in the play. Look at:

- ■ their use of questions
- ■ the way Iago manipulates Othello
- ■ the transition from **verse** to **prose**
- ■ Iago's thoughts on events.

💡 A tragic victim: Desdemona

Very often the characters whom the audience are most sympathetic to in a tragedy are the victims. Desdemona is a victim because she has been framed for adultery by Iago, when she is, in fact, completely innocent, and still in love with Othello.

■ Activity 3

Read this extract from Act 4 of the play, in which Iago, Desdemona and Emilia (Iago's wife) are in conversation concerning Othello's treatment of Desdemona. Consider:

- ■ how Shakespeare presents the frustration of the victim in protesting her innocence
- ■ how Emilia begins to know that Desdemona has been 'set up' by someone.

Study the comments around the text, which should help you to understand the language and how Shakespeare uses it to reveal aspects of the three characters and develop the plot.

There is no commentary with this activity.

■ Did you know?

The first film version of *Othello* was made in 1922. It was a silent movie. In 2001 a television version of the play was made in which Othello was the first black Commissioner of the London Metropolitan Police. *Omkara* (2006) is an Indian film version of the play, set in the state of Uttar Pradesh.

Desdemona is upset because Othello has suspected an affair, and told her off.

This means that Desdemona is not used to being chided (or told off).

This description suggests Desdemona's innocence and how wronged she will be.

This is the main concern of Emilia. She does not like to hear Othello call Desdemona this.

Here, Desdemona calls on the concept of fortune. Fortune is an older medieval concept. The word 'wretched' emphasises her suffering.

'Cogging' is a term meaning deceiving.

'Base' is related to 'bastardry'. It is a concept used by Shakespeare to describe the lowest form of person – the antithesis of a noble hero.

Iago What is your pleasure, madam? How is't with you?
Desdemona I cannot tell: those that do teach young babes
Do it with gentle means and easy tasks:
He might have chid me so, for, in good faith,
I am a child to chiding.
Iago   What is the matter, lady?
Emilia Alas, Iago, my Lord hath so bewhored her,
Thrown such despite and heavy terms upon her
As true heart cannot bear.
Desdemona Am I that name, Iago?
Iago   What name, fair lady?
Desdemona Such as she said my lord did say I was.
Emilia He called her whore: a beggar in his drink
Could not have laid such terms upon his callet.
Iago Why did he so?
Desdemona I do not know: I am sure I am none such.
Iago Do not weep, do not weep. Alas the day!
Emilia Hath she forsook so many noble matches,
Her father, and her country, all her friends,
To be called whore? Would it not make one weep?
Desdemona It is my wretched fortune.
Iago   Beshrew him for't!
How comes this trick upon him!
Desdemona   Nay, heaven doth know.
Emilia I will be hanged if some eternal villain,
Some busy and insinuating rogue,
Some cogging, cozening slave, to get some office,
Have not devised this slander; I'll be hanged else.
Iago Fie, there is no such man! It is impossible.
Desdemona If an such there be, heaven pardon him.
Emilia A halter pardon him and hell gnaw his bones!
Why should he call her whore? Who keeps her company?
What place, what time, what form, what likelihood?
The Moor's abused by some most villainous knave,
Some base notorious knave, some scurvy fellow.
O heaven, that such companions thou'dst unfold,
And put in every honest hand a whip
To lash the rascals naked though the world,
Even from the east to th'west!

Othello, 4.2.109–43

Notice how manipulative Iago is in this sequence. He pretends to care about Desdemona's welfare here.

Note the use of blank verse here. Desdemona speaks using the rhythm of the iambic pentameter.

The text slides across the page here to show that it is a rhythmic follow-on from the previous line ('I am a child to chiding').

Here, Othello has suggested that Desdemona has been having an affair with Cassio, but Emilia suggests he does not have the right information. She still calls him 'my Lord', however.

Iago uses the term 'fair' to describe Desdemona. Shakespeare does this to contrast with Othello's blackness. Iago is also being ironic.

The final word of this line means *drab*.

Iago is role-playing here. He does not really care about her.

These two lines emphasise how important nobility and the hierarchy is within this society.

This is a term of abuse, but Iago will not do this to Othello. He will only continue to make Othello more paranoid.

Here, 'trick' has the meaning of delusion. Iago might be saying this ironically because he knows the delusion he has created.

The word 'office' here is used to mean promotion, but Emilia does not suspect Iago. There is therefore huge dramatic irony in her speech. The audience knows the deceiver is Iago.

This is the most ironic line here – for Iago is the man.

This large-scale image suggests how powerfully Emilia feels about what has been done. The audience feels sorry for her, and goes through pity and fear because they are more aware of events than she is.

Hero, villain and victim: towards climax and resolution

In *Othello*, as in most other dramas, the relationship between the hero, the villain and the victim, and their eventual fates, are worked out in a five-part dramatic structure. Put simply, this is:

- Introduction
- Complication
- Climax
- Understanding
- Resolution.

The second linked extract you looked at above obviously fits into the **complication** stage of the drama, since it is the moment when Iago's plan starts to work, and Othello starts to verbally abuse Desdemona. The tragedy is complicated by this action, and will inevitably lead to the climax (or climaxes) of the drama.

Within *Othello*, there are perhaps two **climaxes** to the action. The first is the point where Othello smothers and kills Desdemona, mistakenly thinking that she has been unfaithful to him; the second is where Othello takes his own life. Both of these sequences are very dramatic and most of the audience would agree that they are where the most tragic moments of the play occur.

After the climax, in *Othello* as in most tragedies, comes the moment where the tragic hero undergoes a process of review and self-evaluation, when they finally **understand** what their fault has been, and how they might have prevented the tragedy from happening. This stage is followed by the eventual **resolution**, which signals the dawn of a new period of time in the imagined world of the play, where hopefully the same mistakes will not be made.

This sequence of climax, understanding and resolution can be seen in the linked extracts from *Othello,* which come from the end of the play. You have already seen Othello's fall from noble hero to rage and incoherence. Look at what he has become now.

AQA Examiner's tip

You may find it useful to apply these five terms to other tragedies because they help to explain the structure and development of a tragedy.

AQA Examiner's tip

It is important for you to remember that tragedy is **drama**, intended to be performed on stage. Whenever possible you should contribute to the practical performance of the text you are studying and working on. Standing up and delivering the lines – or even recording them – will give you a better sense of how the drama operates, and what issues face playwrights, performers, directors and designers.

Link: extracts 3 and 4

To complete Activity 4 you will need to use Othello 5.2.54-108 and 5.2.322-374, which are printed in the Extracts section at the back of this book, extracts 3 and 4.

Link

For a Commentary on Activity 4, see the end of this chapter (p82).

Activity 4

1. What does Shakespeare tell the audience about Othello and Desdemona's thoughts and feelings in the first of these extracts?

2. In this first extract, what is the dramatic function of Emilia?

3. At what point or points does Othello come to an understanding of what has actually happened?

Extension tasks

1. How do the deaths of Desdemona and Othello compare with the deaths of the major characters in the tragedies you are studying?

2. How do you think the original Elizabethan audience would have responded to the deaths of Desdemona and Othello?

■ Interpretations by other readers

Over the years, many **readers** have looked over the tragedy of *Othello* and tried to understand the play better. It is important to remember that the opinions of successive generations of readers about *Othello* are always influenced by the time period they were writing in and by the trends of literary scholarship. For example, someone writing about an interracial marriage in the 18th century would probably have a very different view from someone writing in the 21st century. Therefore, you should read all criticism with a degree of scepticism, keeping an open mind and constantly looking back at the text itself.

Below are extracts from the interpretations of three readers from three different periods.

Early 20th century

> Of all Shakespeare's tragedies, I would answer, not even excepting *King Lear*, *Othello* is the most painfully exciting and the most terrible. From the moment when the temptation of the hero begins, the reader's heart and mind are held in a vice, experiencing the extremes of pity and fear, sympathy and repulsion, sickening hope and dreadful expectation ...
>
> There is no subject more exciting than sexual jealousy rising to the pitch of passion; and there is hardly any spectacle at once so engrossing and so painful as that of a great nature suffering the torment of this passion, and driven by it to a crime which is also a hideous blunder.

A.C. Bradley, 1904

Mid 20th century

> Othello is like a hero of the ancient world in that he is not a man like us, but a man recognized as extraordinary. He seems born to do great deeds and live in legend. He has the obvious heroic qualities of courage and strength, and no actor can attempt the role who is not physically impressive. He has the heroic capacity for passion. But the thing that most sets him apart is his solitariness. He is a stranger, a man of alien race, without ties or nature or natural duties. His value is not in what the world thinks of him, although the world rates him highly, and does not derive in any way from his station. It is inherent. He is, in a sense, a 'self-made man', the product of a certain kind of life which he has chosen to lead.

Helen Gardner, 1963

Late 20th century

This reader, Karen Newman, has spent considerable time exploring the connection between race and sexuality in critical responses to the play over time. One idea that Newman puts forward is that Desdemona appears to enjoy sex with an outsider. Therefore, many prejudices and stereotypes are turned upside down by their marriage:

■ Key terms

Readers: other people who have commented upon or have considered the tragedies we are reading. They may be academics, directors, journalists, reviewers or members of the audience.

AQA Examiner's tip

Your opinion is as valid as those coming from other, more established readers. Do not be intimidated by what they have to say, and always express your view, as long as it is backed up with textual evidence.

> In *Othello*, the black Moor and the fair Desdemona are united in a marriage which all the other characters view as unthinkable. Shakespeare uses their assumption to generate the plot itself – Iago's ploy to string Roderigo along is his assurance that Desdemona could not, contrary to nature, long love a black man. Even his manipulation of Othello depends on the Moor's own prejudices against his blackness and belief that the fair Desdemona would prefer the white Cassio.

Karen Newman, 1987

From this you can see that differences of opinion are part of literary studies. You should also note that tragedies can be viewed from lots of different perspectives: character, structure, problems, cultural, material, identity and gender. Sometimes we will consider criticism from history, and at other times look at more modern interpretations. A range of other readers' opinions helps us to reach our own view of the play.

AQA Examiner's tip

You may like to keep a journal of your own opinions, views and notes on aspects of tragedy, which might directly feed into your coursework explorations.

Group activity

Briefly discuss these three readers' views of *Othello*. Consider the following questions.

1. What differences in the focus of literary criticism do you see over time?
2. Which sentences or phrases seems to sum up the play of *Othello* for you?

There is no commentary with this activity.

Performances of *Othello*

As with readers and critics, performers of different generations have presented different interpretations. All the performances or film versions of *Othello* in some way reflect the cultural, social, political and economic period in which they were produced. This is true of any tragedy, whenever it was written.

However, in some ways the tragedies of Shakespeare and his contemporaries are paradoxically easier to set in different time periods than the domestic tragedies you will read about later. This is because the domestic tragedies are very time- and place-specific.

You may like to try and watch a DVD version of *Othello* to enhance your understanding of the play as a whole. The 1995 film version features Laurence Fishburne as Othello and Kenneth Brannagh as Iago, and you may also discover operatic versions written by Gioachino Rossini (*Otello*, 1816) and Gisuseppe Verdi (*Otello*, 1887).

Did you know?

Shakespeare's Globe is a recreation of the original Globe Theatre in Southwark in London. Not all of Shakespeare's plays were originally performed there, but the theatre gives us a vivid impression of the performance conditions of the period.

Probably the most unusual contemporary production of *Othello* was at the Folger Shakespeare Theatre, Washington, in 1998, when Patrick Stewart played a white Othello among a cast of other black actors. Formerly, white actors (such as Laurence Olivier in a 1964 production at the Royal National Theatre, and Orson Welles in a 1952 film version), would 'black up'. Modern productions of *Othello* at Shakespeare's Globe in London are examples of what is known as 'original practice', emulating how the play would originally have been performed. These different productions have all challenged the way audiences come to understand the tragedy of *Othello*.

Activity 5

Look at the still photographs from two different performances of *Othello*. One is a white actor, Laurence Olivier, wearing make-up and the other a black actor, Laurence Fishburne. Consider the impact each actor's race may have on their intepretation of the role.

There is no commentary with this Activity.

Fig. 1 *Laurence Olivier as* Othello   **Fig. 2** *Laurence Fishburne as* Othello

Ideas for coursework tasks

Essay

Identify two different critical views on an aspect of the Shakespeare play you are studying. Negotiate a title with your teacher that allows you to consider these views and offer your own interpretation.

Commentaries

Commentary on Activity 1

1 You should have noticed that Othello is highly respected by other characters and when he enters he is instantly able to control the action.

2 Most of the other characters on stage give an impression of Othello's greatness by the language they use, but Brabantio refers to him in a very demeaning and racist way.

3 The lines which Othello speaks beginning 'Let him do his spite ...' are very controlled, and despite the abuse he suffers, he refuses to rise to it.

4 At this point, Iago appears to be his friend, but this is all a masquerade, as the audience knows.

Commentary on Activity 2

From the extract link, you should see how Othello is completely overtaken by blind sexual jealousy caused by Iago's villainous scheming. Othello is a very different figure from how he is first presented in the drama (sophisticated, heroic and in control of poetic and witty language). Measured eloquence has now been replaced by incoherence. Notice too in the speech beginning 'Lie with her?' that Othello no longer speaks in verse, but only in prose. Filled with emotional rage, Othello's questions to Iago are short, showing his disintegration and reflecting the disorder and chaos. Iago, meanwhile, is constantly role-playing, offering Othello the answers he wants to hear.

When Othello finally collapses in a trance, Iago uses this moment to offer a short soliloquy to the audience: 'Work on, / My medicine work. Thus credulous fools are caught; / and many worthy and chaste dames even thus, / All guiltless, meet reproach.' The aside is a useful dramatic technique of the tragic villain, which might seem old-fashioned in theatre today, but it is recognisable in many tragedies from the **Renaissance**. It is an insight into the intention and possible motivation of the character at that point, which the audience might otherwise not have known. You should now be able to spot its use in the tragedies you decide to study for your coursework.

Commentary on Activity 4

1   As the tragedy heads towards its climax, Shakespeare tells the audience a great deal about how Othello and Desdemona are feeling. The audience wills Desdemona to survive and understands her protests of innocence because it knows what has been happening. The audience learns how damaged Othello has become from Iago's planning.

2   Emilia is important because she is the only character fighting for Desdemona, trying to prove her loyalty to her husband.

3   By the time Roderigo's letter is found and the plot exposed, Othello has understood how blinkered he has been, and the exact nature of the betrayal. His language here ('O villain!' and 'O fool!') suggests how stupid he has been. The tone alters briefly to a more public style before his suicide ('Killing my self, to die upon a kiss').

Summary

This chapter has given you an understanding of the role of the tragic hero, the villain and the victim, with particular reference to Shakespeare's *Othello*. It has offered you a range of critical responses and interpretations to assist you in arriving at your own interpretation of the play and in applying what you have learnt about these aspects of tragedy in your coursework.

Key terms

Renaissance: period of European history, approximately from 1550 to 1660. The word means 'rebirth'.

Further reading

Shakespeare: Othello Casebook by John Wain (1994)

Othello: Cartoon Shakespeare by William Shakespeare and Oscar Zarate (2005)

Extension (this reading may be challenging)

Post-Colonial Shakespeare, ed. by Ania Loomba and Martin Orkin (1998).

Shakespeare, Race and Colonalism by Ania Loomba (2002).

11 Concepts and theories

Aims of the chapter:

■ Introduces some critical concepts and theories of tragedy, especially those of Aristotle, to enable you to make informed responses to texts.

■ Considers how these concepts and theories apply to the texts you are studying.

■ Key terms

Imitation: in Aristotle's theory, the realistic representation in drama.

Magnitude: great importance or seriousness.

■ Did you know?

Aristotle was born at Stagira in Macedon and lived between 384 and 322 BCE. He was sent to Athens and studied under the philosopher Plato for 20 years, eventually becoming the tutor of Alexander the Great. Through translation, his work became the basis of western education for a number of centuries, though his ideas have gradually come to be seen as old-fashioned. *Poetics* is the exception.

Tragedies may have been performed in other parts of the world in ancient times, but a centre of their production and development was in ancient Greece. In particular, theatrical culture was very advanced in the drama of 5th-century BCE Athens. In Athens during this time, citizens were expected to go to the theatre and drama was seen as an important part of public life. Watching tragedies would therefore be an educational process, because the citizens would learn about codes of behaviour, heroism, what to do and what not to do in life. To an extent, this is true of tragedy in Shakespeare's time and in the 21st century.

■ The theories of Aristotle

One of the most important discussions of the theory or concept behind tragedy is to be found in Aristotle's *Poetics*. In this work, Aristotle attempts to define and understand how the genre of tragedy works. He begins to define tragedy by commenting that a tragic drama is the '**imitation** of an action that is admirable, complete and possesses **magnitude**'. He also notes that tragedy is a form of drama exciting the emotions of 'pity and fear'. Its action should be 'single' and 'complete', presenting a reversal of 'fortune', involving persons 'who are held in great esteem', and it should be written in 'language made pleasurable'.

💡 From these ideas, Aristotle identifies six essential core components in a tragedy:

■ plot

■ character

■ diction (the actual words spoken by the characters)

■ reasoning (the case being staged and the opinions being expressed by the characters)

■ spectacle

■ lyric poetry (a form of poetry through which the dramatist expresses his personal response to the experience being presented on stage).

In such ways, Aristotle established certain features of tragedies, which influenced later Athenian writers, Shakespeare and his contemporaries, and even dramatists writing in our own time.

As you have already learnt, most tragedies are based on a serious exploration of an event that causes the downfall and death of a central character. Remember that in drama, action is generally 'shown' rather than 'told', as it is within narrative. In narrative prose, writers have to explain everything for the reader, but drama is more flexible in its interpretation. Obviously, the way an actor looks at an audience, their facial expressions and their movement and gestures, will give other indications of how the drama is meant to be interpreted beyond the script alone.

You will probably have noticed that some novelists just use dialogue to 'show' what is going on. In this way, novelists use a dramatic method rather than a 'telling' method. 'Telling' in scripts tends to be restricted mainly to the stage directions, but these are primarily for the actors and director.

Novelists such as Thomas Hardy have to rely on chance for narrative to operate. However, according to Aristotle, events in tragedies do not just happen by chance. They happen because of the situations the characters are forced into. From what we know of Aristotle's writings, it seems that he certainly viewed the genre of tragedy as a superior one, at least when compared with comedy. Tragedy was where real truths about human life were revealed, whereas comedy was merely entertainment.

The concept of catharsis

Aristotle further suggested that when writing a tragedy, dramatists should be 'effecting through pity and fear the catharsis of such emotions'. **Catharsis** is the term Aristotle applies to the way Greek tragedies worked – they should purge or sweep away the pity and fear brought about by the tragic action being performed. It is an emotional release that purifies the mind and body. In this way, Aristotle argued, the audience would 'learn' how to behave and run their lives. If you have ever cried during a film or performance, then you will have undergone the cathartic power of that piece of drama. In this sense, the drama you were watching must have been very powerful.

Not all readers and observers of drama agree with the concept of catharsis. The German dramatist and poet Bertolt Brecht (1898–1956) offered a valid argument against Aristotle, which suggested that rather than have the audience purged in this way, tragedies should make people think about how best to alter and change the world. Brecht considered the concept of purification to be an outmoded one. In Brecht's way, tragedies would educate – although judging from some of the observations of Aristotle, he appeared to realise this effect as well; hence why it was considered an Athenian citizen's duty to attend the theatre.

> ### Key terms
>
> **Catharsis:** purification of mind and body brought about by the release of emotions.

> ### Remember
>
> The terms **imitation, magnitude** and **catharsis** were defined earlier in this chapter.

> ### Link
>
> For a Commentary on Activity 1, see the end of this chapter (p86).

> ### Activity 1
>
> Look again at the 'He died a hero' story in Chapters 1 and 9, and the extracts from Shakespeare's *Othello* in Chapter 10. Considering Aristotle's initial theories on tragedy as discussed above, try answering the following questions. Your teacher could project the linked extracts and you could annotate them on a whiteboard.
>
> Alternatively, you could answer the following questions with reference to one or both of the texts you are studying.
>
> 1. Are the two stories an **imitation** of an action that was serious?
> 2. Do the two stories have **magnitude**?
> 3. Are they complete in themselves?
> 4. Do the stories contain persons renowned and of superior attainments?
> 5. Did the stories arouse the emotions of pity and fear in you?
> 6. Did you experience **catharsis**?
> 7. Do you think Brecht's theory of tragedy has some relevance here as well?

The concepts of hubris and hamartia

Aristotle was very clear about the difference between tragedy and other forms of drama. Certainly he saw the 'tragic pity of pleasure and fear' as being the most distinctive thing about a tragedy. Aristotle goes further, however. He notes that in order for the tragic hero to arouse such feelings in an audience, he or she cannot be either all good or bad, but importantly must be someone whom the audience can identify with. Perhaps this is why tragic characters in *Star Wars* or *Lord of the Rings* are so popular.

However, Aristotle believed that if the tragic hero were superior in some specific way (perhaps a king, general, leader, commander or was super-intelligent), then the tragedy and the pity of pleasure and fear would be intensified for the audience watching. Put another way, the tragedy is more intense because the hero has further to fall. In this sense, then, tragic couples such as Romeo and Juliet, or Jack and Rose, have less far to fall than say Tristan and Isolde (who are of royalty), and Othello and Desdemona (who are well-respected in high-class Venetian society). Kings make great subject matter in tragedy because they are at the top of the hierarchy of human society.

Very often, according to Aristotle, the disastrous results are brought about by the tragic hero making a mistake. That mistake, which he calls **hamartia**, is most often based on a tragic flaw in that character. With Othello, it is to put absolute trust in his lieutenant Iago, who is actually spinning a web of deceit. With Macbeth, it is his overambition to become king and then to retain that power in whatever way possible. Aristotle named this tragic flaw **hubris**, a kind of excessive pride that causes the hero to ignore divine or important warnings, or to break moral codes – for example, many characters warn Othello of his self-deception but he chooses to ignore them, or in *Macbeth*, where Macbeth kills King Duncan, breaking the established and 'natural' order.

The critic Karen Newman used the term 'contrary to nature' when she was writing about the marriage of Othello and Desdemona. What she means here is that sometimes tragic events occur because the characters and situations occur which 'invert' or 'break' the natural order. This is related to the **ideology** of the time in which the play was written. In many tragedies the natural order is broken irreversibly. In *King Lear* (which we will look at in detail later on), Lear abdicates and abandons the role of King, dividing up the island of Britain. This inverts the natural order and causes chaos.

It is when the tragic hero's suffering is greater than the actual offence (as in the case of Lear and Othello) that the audience feels pity.

Group activity

Consider the concepts of **catharsis**, **hubris** and **hamartia**. Discuss how relevant you feel they are in the 21st century. Are there any high-status leaders in history, or media stars in the contemporary world, whom we might apply these terms to? Where are these concepts to be seen in the plays you are studying?

There is no commentary with this activity.

The three unities

One final concept of tragedy identified by Aristotle is the three unities. These are **action**, **time** and **place**. Thus tragedies, for their fullest effect, should have action that is sequential, taking place in one day, in one specific place. Put another way, this means there should only really be one plot, though in later forms of tragedies subplots were added to give complexity to the drama. However, you will still see aspects of these three unities in operation, particularly in the drama of Shakespeare and his contemporaries, but also in modern domestic tragedy.

AQA Examiner's tip

The core concepts of **catharsis**, **hubris** and **hamartia** could be part of your critical vocabulary when you discuss tragedies.

Key terms

Hamartia: error committed by a tragic hero or heroine that leads to their downfall.

Hubris: excessive pride or self-confidence which leads a tragic character to commit hamartia.

Ideology: view of the world held by a particular group of people at a particular time. (See Chapter 1 for a definition of the term in the context of a literary text.)

Did you know?

The word 'tragedy' has its origins in the Greek phrase *trago idia* from *tragos* (goat) and *aeidein* (to sing). Tragedy literally means 'goat song'. This may be because songs were sung before goats were led to an altar for sacrifice, or because actors who played satyrs (who featured in early tragedies) wore goat costumes.

AQA Examiner's tip

Build your own glossary of terminology and concepts used to discuss tragedy and the play you are studying. This will be very useful when it comes to writing your coursework.

In theory, the unities of action, time and place should 'compact' the tragedy, with events happening very quickly, in a tight timescale, in the same place. Therefore, the catharsis that the audience should feel is very concentrated. This is certainly the case with 'He died a hero'. If the events were too separated by time or place, then the tragedy might not have the same effect. Shakespeare kept the principles of the unities, but he adapted them slightly to increase realism. A play like *Macbeth* has several different locations, and takes place over a period of time rather than just one day. However, the unities are still recognisable.

Aristotle's theories summarised

Aristotle's theories on tragedy are summarised below. Although they cannot be applied to every tragedy you encounter, the 'model' he suggests is a useful one to keep in mind when you research and write your coursework.

- The protagonist or central character is a man or woman of high rank, power or fortune. The protagonist can be noble (of noble birth) or show wisdom (by virtue of their birth).
- They undergo a catastrophe (Greek: *peripeteia*) – which is usually a reversal of fortune.
- They must suffer beyond what most people ever endure in their lives. Their suffering causes pity (for the protagonist) and fear (in the audience themselves).
- Their downfall is caused by a series of bad choices caused by a tragic flaw in their character. The most common is excessive pride or **hubris**. Often this bad choice inverts the natural order of things.
- There is usually a scene in which the protagonist comes to understand their own flaw and why events have gone the way they have. There is then a recognition of **hamartia**.
- This moment provides the **catharsis** or emotional release for the audience.
- For the fullest effect a tragedy should observe the three unities of action, time and place, with events that are sequential, taking place in one day and in one place.

Activity 2

Considering all that you have learnt so far about tragedy and tragic heroes, take a piece of A3-sized paper, sketch the tragic hero from the tragedy that you are studying, and around and inside the figure draw in all the components that feed into the construction of a tragedy. What you should find is that some of the components are internal and connected with the hero's character (draw these inside the figure), and some are external, connected with events in society (draw these outside).

Present these sketches to the rest of your class. Discuss whether one of these components has an overriding influence, or do they all have an equal contribution to a character's downfall?

There is no commentary with this activity.

Commentary on Activity 1

Othello

Shakespeare's *Othello* is an imitation of an action that is serious. It involves the accusation that Othello's wife is unfaithful to him, and culminates in the death of Othello, his wife Desdemona and a number of other characters.

The play has a certain magnitude: it is set in a rich and powerful city state and contains characters of high social status.

The play is complete. It reaches a full resolution. No sequel is planned because the surviving characters must negotiate their way in the 'new world order' of a Venice without Othello.

Othello is a Moor (one of the play's central issues is that of racism), but he is also a successful military general in the service of the state. Desdemona is the daughter of Brabantio, a Venetian senator – so is also of high status. Therefore they are persons renowned and of superior attainments.

The murder of Desdemona does arouse fear and pity within us as an audience because we know that she is innocent and that Othello is mistaken. Although you have only read and performed a short part of the drama, you should have experienced some of the emotion of catharsis as you worked through the sections. Therefore, the play Othello fits the concept of **epic** or **classical** tragedy.

'He died a hero'

You are probably now beginning to understand that 'He died a hero' is a considerably more modern and domestic kind of tragedy. The story has an action that is serious because the rescue attempt is a serious moment.

The story has magnitude because Steven performs a very heroic task

The narrative is complete in itself: it tells the full story of what happened – before, during and after the rescue attempt – within the limitations on length imposed by the magazine format.

The story certainly aroused the emotions of pity and fear in us, because we realise how close people can be to death.

What makes this story different, however, is that Steven was not a mythical, heroic or grand person. He worked for a refuse collection company, and Patricia, his wife, was a supermarket cashier. However, he completes a deed of extraordinary bravery so is temporarily exalted to the status of a figure like Othello. For this reason you should have undergone the process of catharsis – certainly when you first read the story in Chapter 1.

We can therefore see that both texts fit Aristotle's concept of how a tragedy should operate, even though the stories are many centuries apart.

Ideas for coursework tasks

Essay

To what extent do you believe that the tragedy you are studying integrates aspects of Aristotle's *Poetics*?

Re-creative response

Newspaper editorials often reflect on the lives of great people and the lessons we can learn from them, both from their good qualities and from their weaknesses. Write an editorial that considers the life of a hero you have studied, or write two shorter editorials that view the hero rather differently.

In your commentary reflect on how the newspaper(s) you have chosen for your editorial affects the way you see the hero.

Summary

In this chapter you have been introduced to some critical theories and concepts, especially those of Aristotle, which should allow you to write more confidently about aspects of tragedy.

Violence and revenge

Aims of the chapter:

- Explores the themes of violence and revenge in tragedy, with specific reference to Shakespeare's *Titus Andronicus*.

- Studies aspects of the language used by Shakespeare to express tragic experiences.

- Considers other readers' interpretations of the play in order to inform your own response.

- Considers how the themes you have explored apply to the texts you are studying.

Remember

The **Renaissance** is the period of European history from approximately 1550 to 1660.

By now, you have probably realised that tragedy can sometimes take audiences to the very extremes of human behaviour when the natural order is inverted. In Greek drama there is treachery, betrayal, incest, self-harm, infanticide, suicide and unrelenting violence. Although they are disturbing, gory and bloody, they are not too dissimilar to the kind of subject matter that can be found in many modern horror films. It seems that some of the interest in tragedies is generated from these extreme areas of life.

Titus Andronicus

The earliest tragedy that Shakespeare wrote was *Titus Andronicus*, around 1590. The full title of the work is *The Most Lamentable Roman Tragedy of Titus Andronicus*. Several of Shakespeare's tragedies are given a Roman setting (among them *Julius Caesar, Antony and Cleopatra* and *Coriolanus*). In the **Renaissance**, Roman society and culture was of great interest, so it is not surprising to see so many tragedies set there. It seems that Shakespeare may also have been influenced by the work of the Roman playwright Seneca – in a form of theatre in Roman culture that was performed between gladiatorial conflicts.

Titus Andronicus is Shakespeare's most bloodthirsty tragedy. During his time, it was one of his most popular plays, but fell out of favour over the centuries. However, more recently the play has been re-evaluated and has been performed more often. Initially, readers criticised the play for its violence and the supposedly poor quality of its verse, but recently it has been praised for its vision of 'bleakness' and imagining of the absurdity of life. Today's audiences are perhaps now more used to seeing violence.

Although it does not completely follow the concepts and theories about tragedy outlined by Aristotle and practised by the Athenian dramatists, it does contain many of the elements considered in previous chapters. You might even see the play as a useful bridge between classical Greek drama and tragedy in the Renaissance. You will also find lots of linkages between *Titus Andronicus* and some of Shakespeare's most well-known tragedies.

The bloodthirsty plot

The plot of the play is quite complex, but the principle storyline involves the following. Titus, a respected military commander (who therefore fits the tragic hero model), has returned to Rome after a successful victory over the Goths. Titus brings with him the Goths' Queen Tamora and her three sons. Her eldest son is sacrificed in revenge Titus's own sons' death. Titus is offered the role of Emperor, but mistakenly gives it to Saturninus (the late emperor's son), who is to be married to Lavinia (Titus's daughter).

These events have all kinds of ramifications.

- Saturninus's brother Bassianus claims Lavinia for his own. While attempting to reclaim her for Saturninus, Titus kills his son Mutius who had tried to prevent Titus from acting.

- Saturninus then marries Tamora – providing a disastrous unnatural link between Rome and the Goths.

▦ Tamora's sons Chiron and Demetrius then kill Bassianus, rape Lavinia and cut off her tongue and hands.

At every stage, Titus's world collapses one stage further, and before he comes to 'understanding' he makes many mistakes. Mutilation, death and destruction follow in the wake of his decisions. All of this takes place in the first half of the play!

▦ **Activity 1**

Read and perform the linked extract from *Titus Andronicus*. In this sequence, Aaron (Tamora's lover) asks Titus to complete an ordeal of mutilation. Think carefully about Titus's reaction to events as the scene progresses. How does the language of the scene relate to aspects of tragedy you have learnt about so far?

▦ **Link: extract 5**

To complete Activity 1 you will need to use *Titus Andronicus* 3.1.150–246, which is printed in the Extracts section at the back of this book, extract 5.

▦ **Link**

For a Commentary on Activity 1, see the end of this chapter (p94).

Fig. 1 *Brian Cox as Titus in RSC Production of* Titus Andronicus *at The Swan, Stratford upon Avon, 1987*

🔍 Revenge (1)

Events become even more chaotic in the second half of the play, when Titus, his brother Marcus and his last remaining son Lucius vow revenge. Revenge is an important concept in many tragedies, both in classical Greek drama and in the work of Shakespeare and his contemporaries. Watching characters gaining revenge on those who had done them some harm was popular viewing – and the process of revenge can sometimes form an integral part of a tragedy.

Activity 2

Consider the play you are studying. Are aspects of revenge included within the plot?

There is no commentary with this activity.

The difficulty with revenge is that in a Christian world view, it is regarded as unchristian. Christianity promotes the idea of forgiveness rather than revenge. Revenge is sometimes seen as more of a pagan or Old Testament concept. However, this has never stopped revenge as a central or subsidiary theme in a play being popular with audiences. We all like to see those who have done wrong have their comeuppance – it is a very human trait. Indeed, during the Renaissance there was almost a whole genre of drama devoted to such 'revengers' tragedies', components of which Shakespeare sometimes used in his own work, notably in *Hamlet: Prince of Denmark*.

The linked extract is a revenge-themed sequence from *Titus Andronicus* which begins the final scene of the play. With the help of Lavinia, Titus has recognised his enemies and slit the throats of Chiron and Demetrius. Events now take an even more gory turn.

Link: extract 6

To complete Activity 3 you will need to use *Titus Andronicus* 5.3.1–93 which is printed in the Extracts section at the back of the book, extract 6.

Activity 3

Read the linked extract and answer the following questions.

1. What was your impression when you first discovered that Chiron and Demetrius were to be fed to their mother in a pie?
2. Do you think Titus is justified in his revenge?
3. For what reasons does Titus kill Lavinia?
4. Do you see any similarities here in the way that Aaron and Othello are described?
5. Contrast the language of Titus here with the earlier sequence before he has to cut off his hand.
6. Do you note any language that resembles 'eye for an eye, tooth for a tooth'?

Link

For a Commentary on Activity 3, see the end of this chapter (p94).

Extension tasks

1. Why do you think some readers might be critical of the 'sensationalist' and gory aspects of this tragedy?
2. Many observers say that the language in this tragedy is 'uninspired'. What do you think?

Hint

The term 'sensationalism' is defined later in this chapter.

Revenge (2)

Despite their circumstances, tragic heroes can be very resilient to events taking place around them. Other readers might argue that they are 'blind' to the way their fortunes are proceeding and that to walk away might be a better alternative. Dramatists, however, are keen to show two things: a hero's suffering, but also their bravery in the face of enormous odds against them.

Fig. 2 *Laurence Olivier as Titus Andronicus and Vivien Leigh in Shakespeare Memorial Theatre Production, 1955*

Activity 4

Read the following extract from *Titus Andronicus*. Titus has just received the heads of his sons and his hand, and after a kiss from Lavinia, is in conversation with his son Lucius and his brother Marcus. Marcus urges for action to be taken.

Study the comments around the text, which should help you understand how Shakespeare shows both his hero's suffering and his bravery.

There is no commentary with this activity.

This word is often used to convey lamenting or sad thoughts. It is an exclamation of sorrow.

The concept here is that it is a bad dream that will never end.

This description suggests the age of Titus.

(*Lavinia kisses Titus*)

Marcus Andronicus Alas, poor heart, that kiss is
    comfortless
    As frozen water to a starved snake.
Titus Andronicus When will this fearful slumber
    have an end?
Marcus Andronicus Now farewell, flatt'ry, die,
    Andronicus:
    Thou dost not slumber: see thy two sons' heads,
    Thy warlike hand, thy mangled daughter here;
    Thy other banished son, with this dear sight
    Struck pale and bloodless; and thy brother, I,
    Even like a stony image, cold and numb.
    Ah, now no more will I control thy griefs.
    Rent off thy silver hair, thy other hand
    Gnawing with thy teeth; and be this dismal sight
    The closing up of our most wretched eyes.
    Now is a time to storm, why art thou still?

This is a clever, extended metaphor to explain how Lavinia's kiss cannot comfort Titus.

Marcus takes a much more proactive line here, trying to encourage Titus into action.

This is Lucius, who has been banished from Rome. Lucius eventually becomes Emperor. This is a typical structure in tragedy, where the banished person eventually becomes the leader.

'Wretched is a word often used in tragedy to express how 'low' the heroes have sunk.

Titus explains he cannot cry any more.

'Usurp' is an interesting word choice here. It is usually used in the context of removing a dictator or bad ruler.

Here he asks for the physical power of his family about him.

Hie means 'Go'. Titus is now convinced about seeking revenge and knows he will need support.

Lucius wishes Lavinia had not undergone the mutilation or rape.

'Oblivion' is a common word used by Shakespeare to express the emptiness felt after the events.

Titus Andronicus Ha, ha, ha!
Marcus Andronicus Why dost thou laugh? It fits not
    with this hour.
Titus Andronicus Why, I have not another tear to
    shed:
    Besides, this sorrow is an enemy,
    And would usurp upon my wat'ry eyes,
    And make them blind with tributary tears:
    Then which way shall I find Revenge's cave?
    For these two heads do seem to speak to me,
    And threat me I shall never come to bliss
    Till all these mischiefs be return'd again
    Even in their throats that hath committed them.
    Come, let me see what task I have to do.
    You heavy people, circle me about,
    That I may turn me to each one of you,
    And swear unto my soul to right your wrongs.
    The vow is made. Come, brother, take a head;
    And in this hand the other will I bear.
    And Lavinia, thou shalt be employed in these
      arms.
    Bear thou my hand, sweet wench, between thy
      teeth.
    As for thee, boy, go get thee from my sight;
    Thou art an exile, and thou must not stay:
    Hie to the Goths, and raise an army there;
    And if ye love me, as I think you do,
    Let's kiss and part, for we have much to do.
Lucius Farewell, Andronicus, my noble father;
    The woefull'st man that ever lived in Rome.
    Farewell, proud Rome, till Lucius come again;
    He loves his pledges dearer than his life.
    Farewell, Lavinia, my noble sister;
    O, would thou wert as thou tofore has been!
    But now nor Lucius nor Lavinia lives
    But in oblivion and hateful griefs.
    If Lucius lives, he will requite your wrongs,
    And make proud Saturnine and his empress
    Beg at the gates like Tarquin and his queen.
    Now will I to the Goths, and raise a power
    To be revenged on Rome and Saturnine.

Titus Andronicus, 3.1.251–301

Titus's response here is very human. He laughs at the absurdity of events that have overtaken his life.

Revenge is necessary, but it is also seen as a cave – a passageway with a dark ending.

'Mischief' here is not used in the comic sense. It refers to the serious acts committed to him by others.

This is a very powerful image, which may link with the later importance of eating in the play.

Notice that Lucius describes both his father and his sister as being noble. Their nobility is accentuated by their mutilation.

The language of revenge.

A reference to the ruler of Rome between 535 BCE and 510 BCE, whose reign was characterised by bloodshed and terror.

AQA Examiner's tip

When you come to write your own coursework, you may find it useful to photocopy and enlarge a particularly important scene within the tragedy you are studying. You can then write all of your comments around it, using highlighter pens, underlining and notes.

Interpretations by other readers

Over the centuries, not many readers or observers of *Titus Andronicus* have praised the play. Edward Ravenscroft, an adapter of the play in the 1670s, said that 'it seems rather a heap of rubbish than a structure' and in general there has not been much criticism written about the play, when compared with other more famous tragedies. Below we consider extracts from the comments of two 20th-century readers, Anne Barton and Stanley Wells.

Basically, the tragedy narrows down to one issue: how will Titus, beaten to earth, excluded from the court, deprived of his sons, maddened and maimed, contrive nonetheless to avenge his children? At the end, with most of the cast (including Titus himself) dead by violence, our principal reaction is gratification at the solution of a problem, at symmetry achieved. We can see exactly how, against terrible odds, Titus has achieved his purpose. Questions which go beyond the facts of the case itself are simply brushed aside as irrelevant to this intense, frightening, but wholly arbitrary view of human life.

Anne Barton, 1971

In contrast to Ravenscroft, Barton writes that although there are terrible consequences in the tragedy, a 'symmetry' is reached. This suggestion fits Aristotle's model of tragedy: that it has a purpose or function, and although there has been suffering, this 'symmetry' brings an order to the world again. She also comments that revenge is the principal dramatic motivation in the play.

Stanley Wells offers another perspective, looking at the tragedy in terms of its performance:

[It was a] production of *Titus Andronicus*, by Peter Brook in 1955, that really brought the play back into the repertory and established Titus as a great tragic role. The two principal problems faced by directors of the play are its **sensationalism** and rhetoric. Brooke took care not to overstress the horrors: the severed heads of Titus's sons were concealed in ornate caskets, and Chiron and Demetrius died off-stage. Brooke also evaded some of the challenges of the play's **rhetoric**, cutting over 650 lines including Marcus' description of the ravished Lavinia... Theatrical experience has shown that [the play] has retained its power to move and excite audiences by the opportunities it offers for **pageantry**, by the characterization of major roles... and if they are tactfully presented, by the climactic horrors of the final holocaust.

Stanley Wells, 1987

Wells says several interesting things here. He notes that tragedies come in and out of fashion, and that people now have a new appreciation of *Titus Andronicus*. His comments about how the play can 'move and excite the audience' also seem to be very similar to the comments of Aristotle. We might substitute the word 'pageantry' for Aristotle's term 'spectacle'.

Ideas for coursework tasks

Essay

How important is revenge as a motivating factor in the Shakespeare tragedy you are studying?

Re-creative response

Write a 'transcript' of a talk show in which guests reveal (or hide) information about themselves and their motives.

In your commentary you should aim to explain some of the key moral ambiguities that the play highlights.

Key terms

Sensationalism: use of events, actions, etc. that cause great excitement or scandal. Some directors seek to avoid too much sensationalism in tragedies which involve lots of death.

Rhetoric: the art of using words impressively. In some tragedies in the past, rhetoric is often used, but it can be hard to digest for 21st-century audiences. This is why overly rhetorical lines are sometimes cut.

Pageantry: a public show or procession, sometimes involving people in elaborate costume. Pageantry is dramatically useful because it can show how important the hero is at the start of a drama. *Titus Andronicus* and Sophocles' play *Agamemnon* both begin with pageantry.

AQA Examiner's tip

Build your own glossary of terminology and concepts used to discuss tragedy and the plays you are studying. This will be very useful when it comes to writing your coursework.

Key terms

Duplicity: deceitful behaviour. A character may say they will do one thing, but then commit another act which is treacherous. Most tragedies have moments of duplicitous behaviour.

Commentaries

Commentary on Activity 1

This scene condenses much that you will already have learnt and understood about aspects of tragedy. When Aaron enters, he makes his request in a very matter-of-fact way. Titus's sons will be executed unless Titus cuts off one of his hands. Aaron of course, like Othello, is a Moor and cuts a striking presence on stage. Titus is aware of the **duplicity** of his intent, speaking the words, 'Did ever raven sing so like lark', but at this point still displays heroic qualities. This is reinforced by the words of his son Lucius, who at this highly dramatic point reiterates Titus's achievements ('Stay father! for that noble hand of thine, / That hath thrown down so many enemies / Shall not be sent.'). Lucius and Marcus offer their hands instead, but Titus refuses and allows Aaron to take his own.

The mutilation of Lavinia has already shocked the audience, but this contributes further to the process of catharsis they experience. Titus's speech beginning 'If there were reason for these miseries...' is a classic kind of tragic self-reflection on what has happened to him. He uses powerful images of heaven, earth, sea and flooding, and says that he 'must vomit' his woes. It is significant that at this point a messenger enters, carrying the heads of his two sons, as well as his hand ('in scorn, to thee sent back –'). Titus therefore has been duped by Aaron, further heightening the tragedy. As Marcus says, 'These miseries are more than may be borne.'

Commentary on Activity 3

1   Having learnt that Chiron and Demetrius were to be fed to their mother in a pie, your first impression is probably one of shock and disbelief, but you might also admire Titus's ingenuity and ability to gain revenge upon Tamora.

2   Possibly Titus is justified in his revenge, although if he had not made such poor decisions earlier on in the drama, events would not have come to this.

3   He has to kill Lavinia because she is shamed, and it will also prevent her from suffering further.

4   Lucius's speech here describes Aaron in a very similar to way to Othello: 'Barbarous Moor' and 'accursed devil'. However, the way Lucius describes Aaron is more justified than the way Othello is described.

5   Paradoxically here, in his language, Titus seems much less panicked than earlier on in the play. He even seems to enjoy teasing Tamora: 'Why, there they are, both baked in this pie.'

6   This scene does contain language similar to 'eye for an eye, tooth for a tooth'. Look at Lucius's words, 'death for a deadly deed'.

Summary

This chapter has introduced you to the themes of violence and revenge in tragedy, with particular reference to Shakespeare's *Titus Andronicus*. It has given you an understanding of some of the language used by Shakespeare to express tragic experiences, and has offered you a range of critical responses to assist you in arriving at your own interpretation of the play and in applying what you have learnt about these aspects of tragedy to your coursework.

13   Order and disorder

Aims of the chapter:

- Explores the themes of order and disorder in tragedy, with reference to Shakespeare's *Hamlet* and Marlowe's *Dr Faustus*.

- Analyses the way in which the language of the plays contributes to our understanding of the order and disorder within them.

- Considers how the themes you have explored apply to the texts you are studying.

You will know by now that the shift from order to disorder, and finally back to order again, is a structural feature of most tragedies, in particular those written by Shakespeare and his contemporaries. In this chapter you will consider the complexity of the disorder caused by events in two famous tragedies: *Hamlet* by William Shakespeare and *Dr Faustus* by Christopher Marlowe. These two plays have quite different structures, but are very interesting examples of how playwrights have expanded and developed the genre of tragedy. Thinking about both these dramas should help you to look for issues of order and disorder in the tragedy that you are studying.

 Hamlet

The Tragical History of Hamlet: Prince of Denmark (1600) is probably the most famous tragedy ever written. It is a very long play and in many ways is a kind of revenger's tragedy of the sort you explored when looking at *Titus Andronicus*. The plot of the play is simple: Prince Hamlet listens to his father's Ghost telling him that he (the father) was murdered by his own brother Claudius, now king, and by his own wife Gertrude, now Claudius's queen. Hamlet wishes to obtain justice and revenge for the **regicide**.

The premise of the play, therefore, is that order in the court of Denmark has broken down, as a result of the murder of the King, and until this issue is resolved, disorder will reign. What makes *Hamlet* such a compelling tragedy is that this political and social disorder affects Hamlet in a very personal and psychological way, prompting him to reflect on a number of issues, including love, murder, revenge and death.

Hamlet's indecision and delay in completing the revenge is his fatal flaw. His own personal disorder then creates further chaos for additional characters, resulting in multiple deaths.

Hamlet's desire to expose Claudius and obtain a public confession of his guilt becomes obsessive, causing him to have moral tunnel vision. He inevitably becomes part of the very sickness he is trying to cure – an ironical situation because Claudius is already racked with guilt.

Hamlet tries a number of schemes in order to expose Claudius. Think about these, and consider whether they help Hamlet to achieve this aim and restore order or contribute further to the disorder.

1   He begins an elaborate charade of madness, which is intended to 'make the mad guilty' and therefore cause Claudius to confess.

2   He arranges for a troupe of players to mount a play called *The Murder of Gonzago*. This **play-within-the-play**, which begins with a **dumbshow**, shows the murder of a king in the same way that Hamlet's father was murdered. When it is being performed and one of the actors pours poison into the stage king's ear, Claudius breaks off into a fury.

3   He has the chance to kill Claudius when he is at prayer, but (in line with the Christian world view reflected by the play) Hamlet draws back from the murder because he thinks Claudius might go straight to heaven if he kills him at prayer.

Key terms

Regicide: the killing of a king.

Play-within-the-play: a short play, sometimes a dumbshow, presented in the course of the main action. Several plays from the Renaissance use this convention to elaborate on the themes of the main play.

Dumbshow: a dramatic convention of the period whereby a story is told in silent action or mime.

4   Worried about the duplicity of women, Hamlet alarms and insults Ophelia, his love, treating her with callous indifference and calling her a harlot. Ophelia is the innocent victim in all the disorder and eventually goes mad and commits suicide. Her father Polonius wants to protect Ophelia from Hamlet, but inadvertently contributes to the disorder.

5   Hamlet mistakenly stabs Polonius, causing Polonius's son (and Ophelia's brother) Laertes to seek revenge. Laertes is the opposite of Hamlet. He knows what must be done and attempts to kill Hamlet, but in the end, he too, is fatally wounded.

Activity 1

One constructive way of thinking about the structure of tragedy is to record the steps along the way that contribute to and increase the disorder beyond the original error. In some tragedies this works like a line of dominoes toppling over. Trace the steps that lead to the 'toppling of dominoes' in one of the tragedies that you are studying.

There is no commentary with this activity.

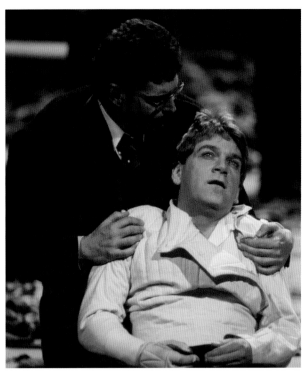

Fig. 1 *Kenneth Brannagh in* Hamlet

The language of order and disorder

As you have probably realised by now, with some dramatists we may have to read several speeches to understand the full nature of what is being discussed in a particular tragedy, but in Shakespeare we can understand a great deal just from reading a few lines. This is because he invests so much meaning in so few lines.

He often seems to say in his tragedies that life could be better ordered, but that characters have to face up to the reality that it will not be. Hamlet's soliloquies are some of the best-known speeches that confront

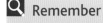
Remember

A **soliloquy** is a speech in which a character tells or confesses their thoughts to the audience, allowing the audience to gain insight into the character's motivation.

this issue. At first glance, these soliloquies about the nature of order and disorder might seem long and ponderous, but they are actually extremely focused speeches which debate major issues.

 Activity 2

You will probably know the opening line of this speech. Read the full speech and annotate the text, explaining how the language relates to the wider issues of order and disorder explored in the play.

Link

For a Commentary on Activity 2, see the end of this chapter (p101).

> **Hamlet** To be, or not to be, that is the question:
> Whether 'tis nobler in the mind to suffer
> The slings and arrows of outrageous fortune,
> Or to take arms against a sea of troubles
> And by opposing end them. To die—to sleep,
> No more; and by a sleep to say we end
> The heart-ache and the thousand natural shocks
> That flesh is heir to: 'tis a consummation
> Devoutly to be wish'd. To die, to sleep;
> To sleep, perchance to dream—ay, there's the rub:
> For in that sleep of death what dreams may come,
> When we have shuffled off this mortal coil,
> Must give us pause—there's the respect
> That makes calamity of so long life.
> For who would bear the whips and scorns of time,
> Th'oppressor's wrong, the proud man's contumely,
> The pangs of dispriz'd love, the law's delay,
> The insolence of office, and the spurns
> That patient merit of th'unworthy takes,
> When he himself might his quietus make
> With a bare bodkin? Who would fardels bear,
> To grunt and sweat under a weary life,
> But that the dread of something after death,
> The undiscover'd country, from whose bourn
> No traveller returns, puzzles the will,
> And makes us rather bear those ills we have
> Than fly to others that we know not of?
> Thus conscience does make cowards of us all,
> And thus the native hue of resolution
> Is sicklied o'er with the pale east of thought,
> And enterprises of great pitch and moment
> With this regard their currents turn awry
> And lose the name of action.

Hamlet, 3.1.56–88

Did you know?

The name 'Hamlet' comes from the Old Norse word *Amlôi*, which means someone who pretends to be dim-witted.

💡 Laughing in the face of death

One of the most powerful scenes in *Hamlet* is the one where Hamlet meets two gravediggers at work. At this point in the play, Hamlet is confronting some of the worst kinds of disorder human beings can face. Death, in particular, is the form of disorder most feared. However, one technique that Shakespeare and a number of other dramatists use is to confront this fear through small moments of comedy, so that the play seems to draw back for a short while from the inevitable and very intense tragic scenes.

Key terms

Pun: a play on words for comic effect.

Necromancer: someone who predicts things by communicating with the dead.

On one level this is simply a way of pausing the action, so that the audience has a break from the intensity of the experience, but the use of comedy also has a bearing on the issue of order and disorder explored elsewhere in the play. Sometimes, black comedy helps to put things into perspective, and we know that even in the direst situations a joke can help. Consider the following sequence, which is full of **puns** and word games:

> **Hamlet** I will speak to this fellow.—Whose grave's this, sirrah?
> **Gravedigger** Mine, sir.
> (Sings) *O a bit of clay for to be made—*
> **Hamlet** O think it be thine indeed, for thou liest in't.
> **Gravedigger** You lie out on't, sir, and therefore 'tis not yours. For my part, I do not lie in't, yet it is mine.
> **Hamlet** Thou dost lie in't, to be in't and say 'tis thine. 'Tis for the dead, not for the quick: therefore thou liest.
> **Gravedigger** 'Tis a quick lie, sir, 'twill away again from me to you.
> **Hamlet** What man dost thou dig it for?
> **Gravedigger** For no man, sir.
> **Hamlet** What woman then?
> **Gravedigger** For none neither.
> **Hamlet** Who is to be buried in't?
> **Gravedigger** One that was a woman, sir; but rest her soul, she's dead.

Hamlet, 5.1.110–28

AQA Examiner's tip

Sometimes, using brief quotations from a play can help you to build up an argument better than longer quotations. You do not always need to quote long speeches in your coursework.

Group activity

Look at one of the tragedies you are studying and discuss the following questions in your group.

- Is there a moment when 'comedy' breaks out and relieves the tension?
- Does the comedy help to illuminate the larger themes of the play?
- Can laughter be seen as a method of dealing with the disorder that tragedy presents to us?

There is no commentary with this activity.

Dr Faustus

The Tragical History of Dr Faustus was written by Christopher Marlowe (1564–93) in 1593. It is another play that considers the issues of order and disorder, but in an innovative way. It is a dramatisation of a legend that was widely circulated in Europe in the later medieval period, concerning a man who sells his soul to the devil. In the legend Dr Faustus is a magician and **necromancer**, but in the tragedy he becomes a man who wants infinite power and his ambition is no less than to become Emperor of the World.

Faustus is frustrated with the conventional order of the world (at this time, the growing interest in science) and so invokes disorder. He calls up Mephistophilis, the Devil, and makes a deal with him in return for 24 years of his life. Mephistophilis provides Faustus with whatever he wants, including the beautiful figure of Helen of Troy. In the end, however, the Devil comes to collect his soul. So the pact that Faustus makes is fulfilled later in the drama with disastrous consequences. Here, instead of debate and discussion as we see in *Hamlet*, the audience watches Faustus make his demands, with a sense of inevitability that some day soon the Devil will collect.

The play reinforces conventional Christian belief: that the ultimate disorder is the Devil or Satan, the original individual who **subverted** the order in the Garden of Eden. However, in this context human beings are the instigators of sin by trying to gain the upper hand in the God-given order of the world. The flaw in Faustus is similar to the flaw in Macbeth: that of overambition and greed. *Dr Faustus* is interesting because it is not about a hero who is a king or a prince, but an ordinary man. Faustus's tragedy is of a spiritual rather than a material nature: he surrenders his **integrity** in order to gain power. Again, like *Hamlet*, this looks forward to the concerns of more modern tragedies.

The tragic hero as villain

Dr Faustus fits into a new type of tragic hero – the kind who is both a hero and a villain. These kinds of tragic hero come to embrace disorder by their actions, which are usually motivated by greed, jealousy, lust and ambition. All these factors motivate Dr Faustus, and by following them he breaks the normal order of the world.

You may encounter tragic heroes operating as villains in a number of tragedies and other types of play. For example, in Shakespeare's history play *Richard III*, Richard is presented as a tragic hero–villain because he plots greedily towards achieving his ambitions. Such characters follow 'nature' too readily and tend to ignore 'civilised' behaviour. Look at the following table showing how a move away from order leads to tragedy.

Order	Disorder
Orthodox behaviour	Unorthodox behaviour
Goodness	Evil
Aware of self	Self-conceited
Peaceful actions	Violent actions
Ignoring temptation	Following temptation
Tradition	Subvert tradition
Live within one's means	Greed and ambition
Natural passion controlled	Natural passion unrestricted
Not coveting others	Jealousy
Seven deadly sins avoided	Seven deadly sins embraced
Accepting God's order	Rebelling against that order
Christian	Pagan
Grace and mercy	Despair and judgement
Repentance	Damnation

Part of the reason for writing tragedies, therefore, is to offer the audience a sense of what value systems are important to us as human beings, and which systems we should try to prevent from taking a hold. This reflects both Aristotle's theories about the importance of watching tragedies in order to learn how to behave and Bertolt Brecht's emphasis on how tragedy can educate and help society to change.

Use of a chorus

The tragic themes of the ancient classical tragedies of Greece were sometimes emphasised by the use of a chorus. The chorus commented upon the disorder being generated by the narrative, and helped explain it

Key terms

Subvert: to overthrow and to turn established order upside down.

Integrity: a person's self-worth and honesty.

Link

See Chapter 11 for a fuller discussion of Aristotle's and Brecht's theories of tragedy.

Did you know?

Christopher Marlowe was involved in a street fight which ended in the death of a man. He was deported from the Netherlands for trying to issue forged gold coins, and was killed in a tavern after a quarrel over a bill.

to the audience. Writers in the Renaissance period, such as Marlowe and Shakespeare, also used choruses to help the audience interpret the play. Shakespeare uses a chorus in his history play *Henry V* for this purpose, but in *Dr Faustus* Marlow uses a chorus both to open the play and to comment upon the action at the end. These passages can be useful to look at because they often summarise and compact the meaning of the play for you.

■ Activity 3

Read the Chorus at the start of *Dr Faustus* (the Prologue) and at the end of the play (the Epilogue). Then answer the following questions:

1 Is a little learning a dangerous thing? Why might this be so?

2 Why do you think Marlowe asks the audience to regard Faustus's hellish fall?

3 Are you reminded of any mythological stories here?

4 What language is particularly powerful in these speeches and why?

5 Some people in our society find order unappealing. Is the move away from orthodoxy and order attractive? You may like to think about tragic rebels in our society.

The Prologue

Chorus So much he profits in divinity,
The fruitful plot of scholarism grac'd.
That shortly he was grac'd with doctor's name,
Excelling all, and sweetly can dispute
In th' heavenly matters of theology;
Till, swollen with cunning of self-conceit.
His waxen wings did mount above his reach,
And, melting, heavens conspir'd his overthrow;
For, falling to a devilish exercise,
And glutted now with learning's golden gifts,
He surfeits upon cursed necromancy;
Nothing so sweet as magic is to him,
Which he prefers before his chiefest bliss:
And this the man that in his study sits.

The Epilogue

Chorus Cut is the branch that might have grown full straight,
And burned is Apollo's laurel bough
That sometime grew within this learned man.
Faustus is gone: regard his hellish fall,
Whose dreadful fortune may exhort the wise
Only to wonder at the unlawful things,
Whose deepness doth entice such forward wits
To practise more than heavenly power permits.

Dr Faustus

Essay

1 How are aspects of disorder developed in the tragedy you are studying?

2 The disorder of the society is matched by the mental disorder of the tragic hero. To what extent is this true of the tragedy you are studying?

Re-creative response

Take a minor character (or characters) from the tragedy you are studying and expand their roles and experiences into a new drama or story, which comments on the original play.

■ Commentaries

Commentary on Activity 2

There is a great deal packed into this speech concerning disorder and order. Hamlet is pondering what actions should be taken and whether he should suffer in silence or confront 'a sea of troubles' and 'by opposing end them'. Death – the ultimate disorder – is considered in detail. It is described as 'sleep', but also as 'the undiscover'd country'. Hamlet refers to aspects of order – 'love', 'law', 'office' and 'patient merit' – but these are described in negative terms. Sometimes, thinking about things too much can 'make cowards of us all'.

You can see that the actual words and language used in this play are very important. In established revenge tragedies like *Titus Andronicus*, the whole emphasis is on the plot and the enactment of the revenge. Here, however, there is new interest in the difference between the thought of doing something and actually doing it. All the time there is an incredible fluency about Hamlet's language, but matching this is a kind of physical paralysis.

It seems that the disorder surrounding the character causes not only this intense self-reflection but also the inability to act. In a way, the audience is willing the character to act, and that is why a tragedy like this is so powerful. The audience is frustrated, but at the same time gripped by his inability to do anything about the situation. This inability to sort through the disorder will be a theme that you will see in modern domestic tragedies where characters are unable to make the necessary change to avoid death and catastrophe. In this respect *Hamlet* looks forward to later tragedies.

Commentary on Activity 3

1 It appears that learning can be a dangerous thing because the person with learning dabbles in things that they should not. For the audience this might reinforce the notion that being 'too bright' might be dangerous and subvert the order.

2 The audience is asked not just to 'look' or 'watch' his fall, but to 'regard' it. If the audience regards Faustus's life in detail, they will learn something about their own lives. In short, Faustus's life is not to be copied or admired.

3   Maybe you will have remembered the story of Icarus here, a man who
    flies too close to the sun.

4   The language of the Chorus is particularly powerful in emphasising
    the tragedy: 'Cut is the branch that might have grown full straight' – a
    line that is applicable to many tragic heroes. There is also a warning
    to those 'swollen with cunning of self-conceit'.

5   Paradoxically, we do find those who choose not to follow the usual
    order of our society the most interesting individuals. Therefore
    'rebellion against the order' is attractive, and this must be part of the
    appeal of tragedies like *Dr Faustus*.

Summary

In this chapter you have considered two important tragedies and have
examined the way in which order and disorder are shaped within them,
including the use of language. You have learnt that in most tragedies there
comes a point where order is destroyed by someone's actions, and then
disorder reigns for much of the play, often intensified by the actions or
stupidity of the main character.

14   Epic and domestic tragedies

Aims of the chapter:

- Explores the different characteristics of epic and domestic tragedies, with particular reference to Shakespeare's *King Lear* and Ibsen's *Hedda Gabler*.

- Analyses comparable sequences from each play, in order to develop your understanding of the similarities and differences between epic and domestic tragedy.

- Explores a range of themes specific to each play.

- Applies what you have learnt to the tragedies you will study for your coursework.

Key terms

Dramatis personæ: the list of characters in a play, found at the start of the script.

Setting: the location where the tragedy takes place.

Illegitimate: born of parents who are not married to each other.

Defining epic and domestic tragedies

We have already learnt that the simplest definition of a tragedy is a play that usually ends with the death of the main character. There are two main types: the type written by Shakespeare (and by the classical dramatists, in which we witness a terrible disorder in a society, and a narrower domestic type of tragedy, which was established by playwrights like Henrik Ibsen in the 19th century, which focuses on the breakdown of a family.

Here are the **dramatis personæ** and **settings** from two tragedies. The first is from William Shakespeare's *King Lear*, written in 1605. The second is from Henrik Ibsen's *Hedda Gabler*, written in 1890.

King Lear	*Hedda Gabler*
Lear, *King of Britain*	George Tesman, *research graduate*
King of France	Hedda Tesman, *his wife*
Duke of Burgundy	Miss Juliana Tesman, *his aunt*
Duke of Cornwall, *husband to Regan*	Mrs Elvsted
Duke of Albany, *husband to Goneril*	Judge Brack
Earl of Kent	Eilert Loevborg
Earl of Gloucester	Bertha, *a maid*
Edgar, *son to Gloucester*	*Scene: Tesman's villa in a fashionable part of town*
Edmund, *Gloucester's* **illegitimate** *son*	
Curan, *a courtier*	
Oswald, *steward to Goneril*	
Old Man, *tenant to Gloucester*	
Doctor	
Fool	
An Officer, *employed by Edmund*	
Gentleman, *attendant on Cordelia*	
Herald	
Servants to Cornwall	
Goneril, *daughter to Lear*	
Regan, *daughter to Lear*	
Cordelia, *daughter to Lear*	
Knights of Lear's train	
Officers	
Messengers	
Soldiers	
Attendants	
Scene: Britain	

Link

For a Commentary on Activity 1, see the end of this chapter (p112).

Activity 1

Study the two lists with a partner. Try to answer the following questions.

1. What do the two lists tell you about the differences in the two plays?
2. Which character do you think is the tragic hero or heroine, and why?
3. What relationships do you think this character has with the other characters of the play?
4. Can you predict what goes wrong?
5. In *King Lear*, look at the characters of Edmund and the Fool. What do you think their role in the drama might be?
6. In *Hedda Gabler*, look at the characters of Bertha and Judge Brack. What do you think their function in the drama might be?

 You will have seen from Activity 1 that there are clear differences between epic and domestic tragedy. Below is a list of the characteristics we might expect to find in these two types of tragedy.

Table 1

Epic tragedy	Domestic tragedy
Ambitious	Seemingly less ambitious
Stresses the nobility of the tragic hero	Focuses on the family
Raises fundamental questions about life	Undermines our confidence in any order
Shows the full horror of life	Shows that domesticity can be corrupt and diseased
Conventional social bonds are broken	Rational social order is no longer maintained
Focuses on the hero	Focuses on the **anti-hero**

Key terms

Anti-hero: a character who does not fit the normal model of heroism.

Activity 2

Think about some of the films and contemporary events discussed in Chapter 9. Which of these types of tragedy do they fit?

There is no commentary with this activity.

You may have noted many similarities between epic and domestic tragedy. In both:

- some act takes place that disrupts society
- the social concord is broken and more violent elements take over
- with order gone, the worst face of humanity is exposed
- the hero or anti-hero has to confront these issues
- one of more of the characters move towards death.

The two case studies below, focusing on comparable scenes from *King Lear* and *Hedda Gabler*, provide an opportunity to examine the different ways in which they are treated.

1 Case study

King Lear

In this play, King Lear **abdicates** as ruler of Britain, a clear alteration in the social order. His good daughter Cordelia is banished and Lear hands over his responsibilities to his evil daughters Goneril and Regan. A vicious power struggle develops and Lear is driven out of doors into a storm. He confronts a chaotic universe in which the state, family, nature and reason have all been thrown into confusion. He asks whether there is any justice or order in the world, whether there is anything that distinguishes human beings' behaviour from that of animals. Lear goes mad, but in lots of ways is clear-sighted for the first time in his life.

Read the following extract, in which Lear enters with the dead body of Cordelia and addresses the Duke of Albany:

> **Lear** And my poor fool is hang'd! No, no, no life!
> Why should a dog, a horse, a rat have life,
> And thou no breath at all? Thou'lt come no more,
> Never, never, never, never, never!
> Pray you, undo this button: thank you, Sir.
> Do you see this? Look on her, look, her lips,
> Look there, look there!

King Lear, 5.3.304–9

This is a very tragic speech. Lear learns of the death of his Fool, as well as having to hold his dead daughter's body.

Questions

In pairs, answer the following:

1. How should these lines be spoken?
2. How do you react to the repetition of some words?
3. Do you think this scene could be overacted? How would you avoid this?

> **Key terms**
>
> **Abdicate:** to renounce or give up a throne.

Fig. 1 *Arubert Reimann as King Lear – English National Opera, 1989*

2 Case study

Hedda Gabler

Now look at this sequence from Ibsen's *Hedda Gabler*, the final lines of the play. Critics have likened *Hedda Gabler* to 'as an early Quentin Tarantino movie ... Hedda was the first chick with guns'. When this play was first performed, it caused a storm of protest, because the play is filled with sexual intrigue, and because Hedda commits suicide, rejecting her domestic role and pregnancy. She is also being blackmailed by Judge Brack. We can see now that it is one of the first plays to depict a very strong female character undergoing the 'tragic process'. It is, however, her husband George Tesman who is left to pick up the pieces.

Hedda (*loud and clear*) Yes, that'll suit you, won't it Judge? The only cock on the dunghill.
(*A shot is heard from the rear room. Tesman, Mrs Elvsted and Judge Brack start from their chairs.*)
Tesman Oh, she's playing with those pistols again.
(*He pulls the curtains aside and runs in. Mrs Elvsted follows him. Hedda is lying dead on the sofa. Confusion and shouting. Bertha enters in alarm from the right.*)
Tesman (*screams at Brack*) She's shot herself! Shot herself in the head! Fancy that!
Brack (*half-paralysed in the armchair*) But, good God! People don't do such things.

Hedda Gabler, from Act 4

Questions

In pairs, compare this sequence with the one from *King Lear*. Then answer the following questions:

1 Which one do you find most effective?

2 How would you suggest the last lines here should be spoken?

3 How do you respond to Tesman's reaction here?

Activity 3

Choose a speech from one of the tragedies you are studying. Transfer 20 lines or so onto a slide using appropriate software. Annotate the speech, showing whether it comes from an epic or domestic tragedy, and how it displays some of the characteristics you have learnt about so far in this chapter.

There is no commentary with this activity.

By now you have probably noticed that tragedies not only involve the death of one or more of the main characters, but also consider a range of related themes as they progress Some tragedies also have a **sub-plot**, which complicates the drama and allows the dramatist to explore other aspects of tragedy. This is true both of epic tragedies by Shakespeare and his contemporaries and of domestic tragedies. We will now take a closer look at these aspects of *King Lear* and *Hedda Gabler*.

Theme and sub-plot in *King Lear*

The sub-plot

The sub-plot in *King Lear* focuses on another old man, Gloucester, who is the father of the illegitimate Edmund. In the drama, Gloucester's eyes are ripped out (an event which reminds us of the blood-revenger tragedies like *Titus Adronicus*) as a punishment for helping King Lear. The audience thus witnesses another character going through the same anxiety and pain as the tragic hero, which intensifies their awareness of the world falling apart. In *King Lear*, the sub-plot works as a parallel to the main plot because both Lear (who has gone mad) and Gloucester have to struggle towards Dover: Lear to escape his evil daughters, Gloucester to kill himself by leaping off the cliffs. The audience sees both characters progressing through a terrifying world that will ultimately end in death.

> ### Activity 4
>
> Can you identify the sub-plot in the Shakespeare tragedy you are studying? Complete a diagram of the main plot and sub-plot. Link the characters with arrows, showing their relationships and their impact on the main plot and the sub-plots of the drama.
>
> There is no commentary with this activity.

Division, folly and kingship in *King Lear*

In Chapter 13 we looked at how changes in the order of society cause chaos. In *Hamlet*, this process began with the killing of Hamlet's father, and in *Dr Faustus* it started when Faustus made a pact to surrender his soul to the Devil. In *King Lear* it begins when the king announces his intention to divide up his kingdom between his three daughters, an act with political implications even if it does involve his family.

> ### Activity 5
>
> Read the linked extract and, working in pairs, answer the following question:
> - What possible interpretations can be made, at this point in the play, of Lear's decision to give away his kingdom?

> ### Key terms
>
> **Sub-plot:** a secondary plot which parallels events of the main plot of a drama (or novel).

> ### Did you know?
>
> The tragedy of *King Lear* is based on the story of the legendary Leir, King of the Britons, first written down by Geoffrey of Monmouth in 1136.

> ### Link: Extract 7
>
> To complete activity 5 you will need to use *King Lear* 1.1.35–91, which is printed in the Extracts section at the back of this book, extract 7.

> ### Link
>
> For a Commentary on Activity 5, see the end of this chapter (p113).

Did you know?

The playwright Edward Bond (b. 1934) wrote a modern version of *King Lear* called *Lear*, which stressed the physical cruelty towards the characters.

Activity 6

Examine the tragedy you are studying. What is the political background to the play? If the play was written by Shakespeare or one of his contemporaries, does it question the 'God-given' and established order of that society? In what ways does it show this?

There is no commentary with this activity.

Illegitimacy in *King Lear*

In Shakespeare's time – and to an extent, in the dark-age world described in *King Lear* – the bonds of family, hierarchy and heritage were very important. Gloucester's illegitimate son, Edmund, has not been allowed to attend the court of Lear for nine years because he is viewed as 'unnatural'. When Gloucester, who says that Edmund is just as dear to him as his legitimate son, brings him to the court, this is viewed as being disastrous to the order of things. Edmund, however, is a new kind of character in Shakespearean tragedy. In the way that Shakespeare develops him in the play, he is a very modern character, who is not bound by the traditional bonds of allegiance to family, hierarchy and heritage. We might go so far as to say he is almost a tragic anti-hero. He very often shares his intentions with the audience in soliloquies (as Iago does in *Othello*).

In this annotated soliloquy from the first act of the play, Edmund reflects on his illegitimacy.

Annotations (left)	Soliloquy	Annotations (right)

This is the old order of Lear's court. Custom is viewed negatively because it has restricted Edmund's progression in society.	(*Enter Edmund, with a letter.*)
	
	Edmund Thou, Nature, art my goddess; to thy law
	  My services are bound. Wherefore should I
	  Stand in the plague of custom, and permit
	  The curiosity of nations to deprive me,
		This subverts the natural order – since Edmund seems to be referring to a pagan goddess, not a Christian male God.

This refers to the fact that he is younger than Edgar.	For that I am some twelve or fourteen moonshines Lag of a brother? Why bastard? Wherefore base?	This means Edmund has been denied of his rights.
Edmund is protesting against the assumption that he is low and vile just because he is illegitimate.	When my dimensions are as well compact, My mind as generous, and my shape as true,	

He comments that he is just as gallant and courageous as befitting a person of noble birth.	As honest madam's issue? Why brand they us
	  With base? with baseness? bastardy? base, base?
	  Who in the lusty stealth of nature take
	  More complication and fierce quality	

This sequence suggests that he was conceived in an excited and 'lusty' way, rather than in the safety and 'dull' state of the marriage bed. The assumption is that he will therefore have more energy and vitality.	Than doth, within a dull, stale, tired bed,
	  Go to th'creating a whole tribe of fops,
	  Got between asleep and wake? Well then,
	  Legitimate Edgar, I must have your land:
	  Our father's love is to the bastard Edmund
	  As to th'legitimate. Fine word, 'legitimate'!
	  Well, my legitimate, if this letter speed,
	  And my invention thrive, Edmund the base
	  Shall top th'legitimate–: I grow, I prosper;
	  Now, gods, stand up for bastards!
		A fop is a fool.
		
		This suggests the inversion of order that will follow.
		
		Again here, the reference appears to be to pagan gods, rather than the Christian God.

King Lear, 1.2.1–21

In referring to Nature as his 'goddess', Edmund shows that he is unaffected by the old order. He questions why he is treated unfairly and considers in detail the word 'bastard' and what it means. When he says, 'I grow, I prosper', it is as if Shakespeare gives him a sense of himself which we do not normally see in tragedies. However, some readers also see him as a villainous character because he plots revenge against Edgar, Gloucester, Albany and Regan.

Activity 7

1. In the Shakespeare tragedy you are studying, is there a certain character whom you have empathy with? Does that character seem to be more modern in their thinking?

2. The problem that Edmund has to deal with is his illegitimacy. What problem does your character carry with them?

3. In what ways can such characters be seen as a link to the characters of more modern tragedies?

There is no commentary with this activity.

AQA Examiner's tip

You may find it useful to complete a 'character track' for your chosen character. Draw a diagram showing when the character first emerges on stage and what they say. Note several other points along their development and then their final appearance on stage.

Hedda Gabler: a typical domestic tragedy

Usually, in epic tragedy, the larger issues and questions are raised very obviously in speeches like those of King Lear or Edmund. In domestic tragedy, the audience sometimes has to read behind the lines to pull out the maximum meaning of the drama. The themes and issues in domestic tragedy are just as grand and ambitious, but characters do not tend to make the grand, confessional-style speeches that you find in Shakespeare and his contemporaries.

Changes in 19th-century society and theatre

We need to read and understand a domestic tragedy like *Hedda Gabler* with an understanding of some of the fundamental changes occurring in society and in the theatre at the time it was written.

In the 1880s and 1890s a wave of **feminist** thinking and agitation – fiercely resisted by most men – swept across Europe. A new, more independent, kind of woman seemed to many to be emerging. In Britain she was referred to as the 'new woman', and in lots of ways this 'new woman' prefigured the feminist movement in the late 1960s and 1970s. In fiction, the same issue was being looked at by writers such as Thomas Hardy. In terms of our understanding of tragedy we can see that this 'new woman' upset the traditional order of society. Given this, any drama that looked at the theme of the 'new woman' would probably end in tragedy.

In Europe in the 19th century, theatre had been characterised by sentimental and sensationalist storylines, declamatory melodramatic acting and unrealistic, flat sets. Towards the end of the 19th century, many playwrights wanted to write dramas that were more realistic, involving domestic storylines, everyday language and **box-sets**, which resembled real houses and followed the principles of acting suggested and formalised by the Russian theatrical theorist Konstantin Stanislavski (1863–1938). Stanislavski had a major influence on some American writers of tragedy – such as Arthur Miller, Eugene O'Neill and Tennessee Williams. For Stanislavski, it was important for the actors to 'believe in the truth' of the drama and to have a 'naturalness' when in role. This would then enhance the tragedy.

Key terms

Feminism: a recognition of the historical and cultural subordination of women, and the resolve to do something about it.

Box-set: a realistic three-dimensional set, with the fourth wall cut so the audience can see in.

Did you know?

Henrik Ibsen (1828–1906) was born in Norway and is regarded as the founder of modern prose drama. He wrote tragedies for 20 years before his plays were translated into English. He was one of the the first major dramatists to write tragedies about ordinary people.

Fig. 2 *Hedda with the pistol*

The context and plot of *Hedda Gabler*

In 1879, Ibsen had written a play called *A Doll's House*. When it was first performed in Copenhagen many people were shocked, because the play ended with the lead female character leaving her marriage and children behind. It attacked the certainty of marriage and the bond between a mother and her children. Although no one was killed, the play was very radical for its time. *Hedda Gabler* goes one stage further because the play culminates in the pregnant Hedda committing suicide.

Hedda Gabler might be regarded as a typical domestic tragedy because of the way the plot is constructed. Hedda, who is the daughter of the impoverished General Gabler, has just returned from honeymoon with her academic husband George Tesman. Tesman is a boring but economically secure young man, who spent time on their honeymoon completing research. Domestic harmony is thrown into chaos thanks to the reappearance of Eilert Loevborg – a gifted academic, but one who has wasted his talent due to his drinking. Loevborg poses a threat to Tesman as a competitor for the university professorship.

Loevborg has had a relationship with an old schoolfriend of Hedda's, which makes Hedda jealous. Tesman takes Loevborg to a party and leaves him there. Tesman then returns home to find a manuscript of Loevborg's, which he believes he has lost. Hedda then burns the manuscript in order to secure Tesman's future. Hedda has given Loevburg a pistol so that he may take his life heroically. News comes that he is dead, and after the machinations of Judge Brack, Hedda decides to take her own life.

The sub-plot of *Hedda Gabler*

The sub-plot of the play is based around the character of Judge Brack. Brack says that Loevborg's death was messy and accidental, and that he knows that Hedda gave him the pistol. Brack now has power over Hedda, and it is implied that he will use this to make Hedda pay him with sexual favours.

This sub-plot is important because Hedda's main aim was to break free from the **patriarchal society** she finds herself in. All the male characters – Tesman, Loevburg and Brack – put pressure on Hedda to conform. It is significant that such an emphasis is put on Hedda's surname. As a child she was unable to escape the name of her father, and now she cannot escape other men.

Domestic tragedy in *Hedda Gabler*

You can see from the above that the plot of this play could almost come from a Greek tragedy, with two rivals in a love triangle. The time span of the drama is very tight, and the setting is the same throughout. The number of characters on stage is very small, but they are all connected. Hedda is the heroine, but she is more an anti-heroine.

An important feature of domestic tragedy is the slow **revelation** of information to the audience. The audience then works out why particular characters behave in the way that they do. Bertha, the maid, is important since it is she who passes on important information in the play. It is significant that Tesman has spent some of his honeymoon on his research, because the two newly-weds ought to be enjoying time together. It is symbolic of the wider division in their marriage from the outset.

The play has a certain shock value for the audience, because of the way Hedda commits suicide, and because it is an unexpected end to a **well-made play** from this period. By then, though, the audience has already started to experience the main effects of classical tragedy as outlined by Aristotle. However, we presume that only after the play has finished will a character like George Tesman undergo the appropriate cathartic process.

Activity 8

If you have read or watched *Hedda Gabler*, as a way into the creative coursework assignment suggested below you may like to write George's reflections after Hedda's death. This will require some thought, because through the play and probably in its immediate aftermath, George is highly ignorant of Hedda's real needs as a modern woman with an enquiring mind.

Alternatively, choose a character similar to George Tesman from one of the plays you have studied and write their reflections on the aftermath of events. You may, of course, integrate some quotations from the original text.

There is no commentary with this activity.

Other readers' views on *Hedda Gabler*

After the first British performance of the play in 1891, the *Daily Telegraph*'s reviewer wrote: 'What a horrible story! What a hideous play! ... The play is simply a bad escape of moral sewage-gas ... Hedda's soul is a-crawl with the foulest passions of humanity.'

The novelist Henry James wrote of the same performance that it was 'the artistic exercise of a mind saturated with the vision of human infirmities.' James seems correct here. The play is about human infirmities, as are most tragedies. Since his comments, most readers have viewed *Hedda Gabler* in a more positive light, with over 25 productions of the play in London alone.

Hedda herself has been seen in a variety of ways, as:

- an idealistic heroine fighting a patriarchal society
- a victim of circumstances
- an early feminist
- a manipulative and cunning villainess.

Which do *you* think she is?

Feminism in *Hedda Gabler*

It can be interesting to examine a tragedy from a feminist viewpoint. We might apply a feminist literary reading to *Hedda Gabler* because Hedda is a very strong female role for an actress to play, and because she is an example of a new kind of woman emerging in the late 19th and 20th centuries.

Did you know?

In Norwegian, *Gabler* means 'freedom'. Writers of tragedy often name their characters symbolically.

Group activity 1

Read the linked extract, which sees Hedda clashing with George's aunt, and George trying to 'repair' the relationship between them. There is an indication that Hedda is pregnant and also an indication of tragedy to come at the end of the play: 'People don't do such things'.

Annotate the text with your comments and observations.

There is no commentary with this activity.

Link: extract 11

To complete Activity 1 you will need to use the section from *Hedda Gabler* that is printed in the Extracts section at the back of this book, extract 11.

Further reading

M. Egan (ed.) (1972) *Ibsen: The Critical Heritage*, London: Routeledge.

M. Meyer (ed.) (1992) *Ibsen*, London: Cardinal Books.

Group activity 2

Examine one of the tragedies you are studying in the light of feminism. Are there characters ahead of their time? What patriarchal methods of control are in place?

There is no commentary with activity.

Ideas for coursework tasks

Essay

Consider the potential significance of the sub-plot(s) in a play you have studied.

Re-creative response

Imagine that a character in the play you are studying is discovered to have written a series of letters, either to one or to several people. You have been asked to edit a collection of such letters. Prepare the letters for publication in a book, by giving extracts and then adding editorial notes, interpretations, and so on.

Commentaries

Commentary on Activity 1

1   Lists like this can tell us a lot about the nature of these two different kinds of tragedy. You probably noticed that *King Lear* has a lot more characters in it than *Hedda Gabler*. You will also have noticed the differences in location: 'Britain' is the location for *King Lear* – the place is not specified, but it somehow seems 'epic' and 'grand'. The Laurence Olivier version of *King Lear* is set against a backdrop of Stonehenge. The location is much more specific in *Hedda Gabler*. Ibsen not only describes the type of house, but also where it is located in the town.

    The two plays are very different. *King Lear* is an epic tragedy, involving lots of characters, whereas *Hedda Gabler* is tightly focused around one family.

2   You are right to identify King Lear and Hedda Gabler as the tragic hero and heroine of their irrespective plays – after all, the plays are named after them.

3   Did you spot the three daughters of Lear at the bottom of the list and also the fact that they have husbands? It seems they might somehow be significant to the tragedy. If you were reading closely you may have noted that Cordelia has no husband. In *Hedda Gabler* maybe you noticed that both Hedda and Juliana Tesman are described in terms of 'belonging' to George Tesman, with the word 'his' after their names.

4   Predicting what might go wrong is difficult, but you may have picked up that Edmund in *King Lear* is illegitimate ('bastard son'). These days people are less bothered about illegitimacy, but in previous times it was considered a problem because it ran against the natural order of things.

    Perhaps what goes wrong in Hedda Gabler will be to do with the tensions surrounding a relationship and the control of that relationship.

5   As we have seen, Edmund's illegitimacy is likely to be an issue. In plays of this period, fools can often have an insight into events, even though their pretence is to be outwardly stupid and naive.

6   Judge Brack is evidently a man of standing in *Hedda Gabler*, and you are probably aware that servants often contribute valuable information to the plot.

Commentary on Activity 5

One way of looking at this would be to say that what King Lear is doing is giving sections of Britain a sort of devolution (in a way the separate Welsh Assembly or Scottish Parliament have been established in our own time), and that Shakespeare appears to disapprove. When King Lear decides to divide up the kingdom of Britain into three component parts, Shakespeare seems to suggest that this is something 'unnatural' and should not be happening. Division will lead to chaos.

Viewed from a historical context, we know that kings were thought by people in medieval times to be 'God-given', next down in the order of the world from God himself. During the Renaissance, many people were questioning this 'God-given' right of kings, so Shakespeare may be presenting a king who thinks he can play God, but can not really. Folly too will lead to chaos.

Different readers of *King Lear* will have varying views on the play, which will also be influenced by dramatic productions. People who support the monarchy might say that the play eventually shows that we should retain kings and queens. Others might argue that the tragedy shows a political process in which a foolish **oligarch** gets his just comeuppance. Clearly, tragedies consider issues of power and control, essentially political concerns.

Summary

In this chapter we have explored the differences between epic and domestic tragedy and examined two examples in considerable depth. You have learnt that while domestic tragedy has a smaller cast, it none the less focuses, like epic tragedy, on very ambitious themes, and you have explored some of these themes in each of the two plays.

15 Modern domestic tragedies

Aims of the chapter:

- Explores the characteristics of modern domestic tragedies, with particular reference to Miller's *Death of a Salesman*.

- Analyses some of the techniques used by the playwright to express and develop the central themes of the tragedy.

- Applies what you have learnt to the tragedies you will study for your coursework.

Remember

A **modern** tragedy is one written in the late 19th or 20th century, earlier than a **contemporary** tragedy (late 20th or 21st century).

Key terms

Materialism: an excessive regard for material possessions.

Consumerism: contemporary society's obsession with consumer spending on new products and services.

Procrastination: to postpone or put off doing something. Many characters in modern domestic tragedies fail to make necessary changes to improve their lives, and this can contribute to their downfall.

Alienation: a feeling that people experience when the world around them becomes unfamiliar and disorientating.

Remember

A **box-set** is a realistic three-dimensional set.

The characteristics of modern domestic tragedy

You will have some understanding by now of what makes up a modern domestic tragedy. In this chapter you will explore in detail another example of this genre of tragedy, which should show you that although less epic in scale, such tragedies can still be very powerful, and can appeal to contemporary audiences because they deal with 'modern' issues such as **materialism**, **consumerism**, **procrastination** and **alienation**.

Modern domestic tragedy therefore tends to be 'issue-led'. This means that the tragedy looks at a particular issue and examines its effect on the central characters. Like *Hedda Gabler*, most modern domestic tragedies focus on anti-heroes, who do not quite fit the society in which they are involved. Most characters in these tragedies face some kind of predicament.

Modern domestic tragedies can still have the same effects on the audience as those identified by Aristotle (which we looked at in Chapter 11), but they also cause the audience to question established systems and principles and assumptions about life. Some modern playwrights try to subvert 'normal' values in more ways than one, breaking established conventions of drama as well as subject matter. Some plays reflect the horror and tragedy of modern life, and some are fragmented and disordered, reflecting more secular beliefs and the experience of large-scale war and conflict.

Structurally, the plays are usually much more condensed than epic tragedies – most only having three acts. You should also expect to see much more emphasis on exactly what the set should look like, as well as on costuming, sound, lighting, stage directions and how particular sections of the text are to be spoken. This is partly because modern playwrights are more concerned about such details, and partly because of technical advances in the theatre. Most modern tragedies are staged in **box-sets**, although some 20th-century playwrights have tried to use more innovative sets.

Below is a summary of the elements you might expect to see in modern domestic tragedy:

- The central characters are anti-heroes or heroines.
- These characters are ordinary people – not the great men or women of earlier tragedies.
- Although family life is central, it is presented as somehow corrupt and diseased.
- This corruption undermines faith and belief in the whole order of society.
- The world is seen as being full of deceit, and prizes or dreams chased are illusory.
- Often characters vie and manoeuvre for control.
- There is often an emphasis on psychological elements.
- The disorder of the world sometimes matches a disorder of the mind.
- Deaths are usually not shown on stage (as in earlier tragedies), but happen offstage (or are concealed).

Earlier tragedies tend to look 'outwards'; modern domestic tragedies look more 'inwards'.

 Usually, some element of the past impinges tragically on the present.

Activity 1

If you are studying a modern domestic tragedy, look at a small section of the play – perhaps two or three pages. Can you find the above elements in the section that you are considering? If so, make notes about what you discover.

The is no commentary with this activity.

Death of a Salesman

Arthur Miller (b.1915–1920) is one of America's most famous dramatists, and his 1949 play *Death of a Salesman* is an important modern domestic tragedy.

The plot

The play centres on the life of a sixty-something salesman called Willy Loman, who has spent much of his life on the road as a travelling salesman. He seems once to have been liked and well-known, but increasing bouts of anxiety and flashbacks have meant that he has become unstable. In the play, he stands in the shadow of his more successful brother Ben, and is sacked from his job when he requests a post off the road back in New York.

Willy has high hopes of his two sons, Happy and Biff, who were well-liked at school. Happy, the younger son, lies to his father to make himself look like a success. Biff, the older brother, is 34 and is still unsettled and without a career. Willy's wife, Linda, has to struggle to make ends meet, while we learn that in the past Willy had an affair while out on the road, which was observed by Biff.

With a 'get-rich-quick deal' or prospects always on the horizon, but never quite reached, Biff decides to confront his father and tell him the truth. Willy wants to be well-liked, believing that this will bring success and the American dream to him and his family, but in an emotional climax with Biff, he realises his failure and how society has failed him. Willy takes his own life. Put another way, Willy postures and bluffs his way into believing in the **mythology** of success, while drowning in his own failure.

Death of a Salesman and *Hedda Gabler*

As you can see, there are some similarities between these two plays. Willy is somehow dissatisfied with his life like Hedda, but cannot find the power to change it. The relationship with his partner Linda is important, and just as Hedda had a prior relationship with Loevborg, so Willy also has a secret past. The desire for domestic happiness and material goods is important in both dramas, but as an audience we become aware that there is something unstable and deceitful under the surface. The ghosts of the past therefore haunt the present.

Miller's techniques

Flashback

By the time Miller came to write *Death of a Salesman*, cinema had become an immensely important genre, and this tragedy is much

Key terms

Mythology: a traditional tale or belief.

Did you know?

In order to write *Death of a Salesman* in spring 1948, Arthur Miller went to live in a log cabin in Connecticut. When he arrived at the cabin, he had the first two lines of the play in his mind. He emerged six weeks later with the final script.

influenced by a technique commonly used in film: that of a kind of flashback. Flashback allows the playwright to take the audience back in time and observe events that took place before the actual play on stage began. Miller uses this technique throughout *Death of a Salesman*, and deftly manages the transitions between the present and the past, or more precisely the past as Willy remembers it. Miller himself described this method as 'mobile concurrences' or 'simultaneity', whereby the playwright shows subjective memories of a character's past. This is a very modern method of writing, not available to Shakespeare and his contemporaries, and it helps the audience to understand the reasons behind Willy's psychological problems.

Structural devices

Unlike most modern dramas, Miller's play only has two acts – which Miller calls 'Certain Private Conversations in Two Acts' – although there is a third section which is labelled 'Requiem'. This takes place at Willy's funeral and is the new world in which the characters must exist and work, after the death of the main character. Nobody but Willy's immediate friends and family turn up, which shows that regardless of how well Willy thought he was liked, very few people either cared about him or remembered him. Happy thinks that Willy did not die in vain, but Biff comments that, 'He had the wrong dreams. All, all, wrong.' This judgement of Willy can also be seen as a judgement of the wider American wish to be liked, to have material goods and to chase a false dream. In this way, the domestic drama provokes observations on bigger issues and themes.

Irony

In modern tragedy, **irony** is a very important device. The play is filled with ironic lines and observations. In the 'Requiem', Willy's dream of owning his own house is realised, but only after his death (a reference to his earlier observation that he will be 'worth more dead than alive'). Linda has paid the last mortgage payment that morning, but Willy is not there to enjoy this – an outcome that is both tragic and hugely ironic. His death may well 'set up' the boys for a better life. It is a very noble and heroic act – terms that should make you think of earlier tragedies.

Music

Music was used in classical drama and also in the tragedies of Shakespeare and his contemporaries. Miller's *Death of the Salesman* also makes use of music to advance and enhance the tragedy. This is a common technique in film, but is less used in the theatre.

Fig. 1 *Willy and Biff in 'Death of a Salesman'*

Activity 2

Answer the following questions about the modern domestic tragedy you are studying:

1. What organising or structural devices does the playwright use?

2. How do the other surviving characters cope after the death of the main character?

3. Is any music used to enhance the tragedy? If there is no music, do you think its introduction by a director might be effective?

4. Are there moments when the usual dramatic realism is suspended? How is this achieved?

5. How does the dramatist deal with the issue of the past impinging upon and influencing the present?

There is no commentary with this activity.

A compacted time frame

Although *Death of a Salesman* is a modern drama, Arthur Miller was much influenced both by classical drama and by Ibsen when he came to write it. However, he was keen to escape naturalistic drama and the realistic time frame. He wanted to write a tragedy in which memories and anxieties would enter the anti-hero's brain during the course of the play, perhaps paralleling the way people really think and behave. This technique allows Miller to compress everything about Willy into a period of 24 hours. Like Ibsen's *Hedda Gabler*, *Death of a Salesman* begins at a moment of optimism in the family – but events soon turn sour.

Activity 3

Read the following extract, in which Willy is in the present, remembering a happier time in the past when he is having a conversation with his boys. On stage, the older Biff and Happy would be sleeping above. The same characters are therefore on stage at both times in their lives (as children and as adults), enabling Miller to merge the past and the present.

What language indicates that the past was a better time than the present?

Link

For a Commentary on Activity 3, see the end of this chapter (p121).

Willy ... Soon as you finish the car, boys, I wanna see ya. I got a surprise for you, boys.
Biff (*offstage*) Whatta ya got, Dad?
Willy No, you finish first. Never leave a job till you're finished – remember that. (*Looking towards the big trees*) Biff, up in Albany I saw a beautiful hammock. I think I'll buy it next trip, and we'll hang it right between those two elms. Wouldn't that be something? Just swingin' there under those branches. Boy, that would be...
(*Young Biff and Young Happy appear from the direction Willy was addressing. Happy carries rags and a pail of water. Biff, wearing a sweater with a black 'S', carries a football.*)
Biff (*pointing in the direction of the car offstage*) How's that, Pop, professional?
Willy Terrific. Terrific job, boys. Good work, Biff.

Death of a Salesman, from Act 1

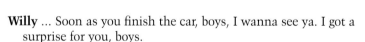

Activity 4

Read and study the following extract from the end of Act 2 of *Death of a Salesman*, which is annotated so that you can see where ideas and issues are being explored.

There is no commentary with this activity.

The dialogue direction here tells the actor how angry the character is. This is a key speech from Biff. He realises and admits to his father that he is a failure in life. However, the implication is that this applies to Willy as well.

Willy still seems oblivious of what is actually going on around him. There is an indication that men should not cry.

This is another important line which refers to the deceit of the American dream and foreshadows Willy's eventual death.

This realisation has been a long time coming, but there is now a shift in the relationship between Willy and Biff.

This comes after Willy should have realised what kind of person Biff is, but still Willy has faith in change.

Think about how the line might be spoken. It could be delivered in an ironic way. Ben has been the successful brother. It is an example of Miller's tyical technique of merging the realism with a memory or voice.

This seems another piece of procrastination – something that will never actually happen.

Biff (*at the peak of his fury*) Pop, I'm nothing! I'm nothing, Pop. Can't you understand that? There's no spite in it any more. I'm just what I am, that's all.
(*Biff's fury has spent itself, and he breaks down, sobbing, holding on to Willy, who dumbly fumbles for Biff's face.*)
Willy (*astonished*) What're you doing? What're you doing? (*to Linda*) Why is he crying?
Biff (*crying*) Will you let me go for Christ's sake? Will you take that phoney dream and burn it before something happens? (*Struggling to contain himself, he pulls away and moves to the stairs.*) I'll go in the morning. Put him – put him to bed. (*Exhausted, Biff moves up the stairs to his room.*)
Willy (*after a long pause, astonished, elevated*) Isn't that – isn't that remarkable? Biff – he likes me!
Linda He loves you Willy!
Happy (*deeply moved*) Always did, Pop.
Willy Oh, Biff! (*Staring wildly*) He cried! Cried to me. (*He is choking with his love, and now cries out his promise*) That boy – that boy is going to be magnificent!
(*Ben appears in the light just outside the kitchen.*)
Ben Yes, outstanding, with twenty thousand behind him.
Linda (*sensing the racing of his mind, fearfully, carefully*) Now come to bed, Willy. It's all settled now.
Willy (*finding it difficult not to rush out of the house*) Yes, we'll sleep. Come on. Go to sleep, Hap.
Ben And it does take a great kind of man to crack the jungle.
(*In accents of dread, Ben's idyllic music starts up.*)
Happy (*his arm around Linda*) I'm getting married, Pop, don't forget it. I'm changing everything. I'm gonna run that department before the year is up. You'll see, Mom. (*He kisses her.*)
Ben The jungle is dark, but full of diamonds, Willy.
(*Willy turns, moves, listening to Ben.*)
Linda Be good. You're both good boys, just act that way, that's all.
Happy 'Night, Pop. (*He goes upstairs.*)
Linda (*to Willy*) Come, dear.
Ben (*with greater force*) One must go in to fetch a diamond out.

This stage direction tells us that this is the peak of the tragedy.

This sounds like a comment made to a child who has been naughty.

Happy seems oblivious to the bigger picture.

Here joyous and idyllic music is used to undercut the real tragedy occurring. This is why Miller wants it to be 'an accent of dread'.

This would be good advice at the start of Willy's career. Willy entered the jungle but found a few diamonds.

Death of a Salesman, from Act 2

Core speeches

As you will have learnt from previous chapters, sometimes the main characters of tragedies make core speeches on which much of the tragedy is centred.

Activity 5

Consider the following sequence of dialogue between Willy Loman and his wife Linda. Then answer the following questions:

1. How does it relate to the central tragedy of the play?

2. In the play you are studying, find at least one similar core sequence of dialogue between the central characters which seems to summarise the issues being considered in the tragedy. Report back to the group with your choices.

> **Willy** Whoever heard of a Hastings refrigerator? Once in my life I would like to own something outright before it's broken! I'm always in a race with the junkyard! I just finished paying for the car and it's on its last legs. The refrigerator consumes belts like a goddam maniac. They time them so when you finally paid for them, they're used up.
> **Linda** (buttoning up his jacket as he unbuttons it) All told, about two hundred dollars would carry us, dear. But that includes the last payment on the mortgage. After this payment, Willy, the house belongs to us.

Death of a Salesman, from Act 2

Other readers' views of *Death of a Salesman*

Death of a Salesman is generally considered to be one of the most important American plays of the 20th century. The critic Ronald Harman says that 'the play is universal because it is particular', suggesting that the very specific setting of characters and place appeals to us because we see something of ourselves in it.

When the play was first performed, Miller reported that:

> As sometimes happened later on during the run, there was no applause at the final curtain of the first performance. Strange things began to go on in the audience. With the curtain down, some people stood to put their coats on and then sat again, some, especially men, were bent forward covering their faces, and other were openly weeping. People crossed the theatre to stand quietly talking with one another. It seemed forever before someone remembered to applaud, and then there was no end to it.

Arthur Miller, Timebends: A Life, *1987*

Watching this tragedy was clearly a very moving experience for the audience. They probably had not witnessed this kind of modern play before, so were unsure how to respond to it. Note in particular the reaction of male members of the audience, who were clearly **empathising** with the situation Willy Loman found himself in. The play was also criticised by some observers as being anti-American because it dared to criticise the American way of life.

AQA Examiner's tip

It is often helpful to take three core 'slices' through the drama you are studying. Wherever you cut your slice through the play, you should be able to bring out the larger themes and issues it reflects, and show how the structure and language contribute to the effect.

Link

For a Commentary on Activity 5, see the end of this chapter (p121).

Did you know?

In 1983 Arthur Miller directed his own production of the play in Beijing, just as China started to embrace westernised capitalism.

Key terms

Empathise: to identify with someone else's feelings or experiences.

■ Other modern tragedies

Below are some brief notes on some other modern domestic tragedies, which follow a number of the same principles of characterisation, theme, structure and language as *Hedda Gabler* and *Death of a Salesman*. These plays also relate the particular domestic issues to wider social and more universal themes. You might like to research and read about some of them.

■ *The Father* (1887) by the Swedish writer August Strindberg (1849–1912). This is a play about a father and a mother vying for control over their child. The man fails and the woman triumphs because of her strength of will.

■ *The Shadow of a Gunman* (1923) by the Irish writer Sean O'Casey (1880–1964). Set in the context of Irish nationalism, this is a tragicomic play about tenement life, self-deception and cowardice.

■ *Yerma* (1934) by the Spanish writer Frederico García Lorca (1899–1936). This tragedy tells the story of a childless woman living in the countryside. Her obsessive desire for motherhood drives her to murder her husband.

■ *Long Day's Journey into Night* (1941) by the American writer Eugene O'Neill (1888–1953). This is a semi-autobiographical family tragedy about the mutually destructive relationships between Mary Tyrone, her ex-actor husband James, and their two sons – the intellectual Edmund and the alcoholic Jamie.

■ *Cat on a Hot Tin Roof* (1955) by the American writer Tennessee Williams (1911–83). This play is a family drama which takes place at Big Daddy's 65th birthday. Big Daddy owns a cotton plantation. His daughter-in-law Maggie tries to save her marriage to failed football hero and alcoholic Brick.

You will notice that there are no tragedies listed here by British writers. That does not mean that tragedies were not written in Great Britain – just that the most famous ones from this period come from other countries. The expansion and development of the USA into a 'superpower' in the 20th century prompted a parallel development in drama which sought to define that experience within the tragic form. British playwrights have also continued to write tragedies. *The Permanent Way* by David Hare (2003) is a tragedy based on the decision to privatise the railway system in Britain, which shows how the events of a rail crash affect individuals and their families.

Tragedies are often written when some social change or progression happens in society. Think of the way in which issues concerned with the rights of women are explored in *Hedda Gabler* by Ibsen and *The Father* by Strindberg.

AQA ✓ Examiner's tip

Always re-read the play you are studying a number of times. You will find that additional themes and issues emerge from a second reading. If possible, try to see a performance of a modern domestic drama. Compare it with the text you are studying for your coursework.

■ Ideas for coursework tasks

Essay

It was noted at the start of this chapter that modern tragedies deal with modern issues such as materialism, consumerism, procrastination and alienation. To what extent does the modern tragedy you are studying show evidence of at least two of these issues, and how does the playwright present them?

Re-creative response

A coroner is a court official who deals with causes of death. Write the summing-up speech made by the coroner at the end of an inquest on the deceased character in the modern tragedy you are studying.

In your commentary discuss the extent to which the play suggests that 'causes of death' can be defined.

Commentaries

Commentary on Activity 3

The past that Willy is remembering seems a better time, but there is still the concern with material goods (the hammock) and the desire to complete something that will probably never happen (to put it between the elms).

The language here is important. Willy's words 'that would be...' are crucial in understanding him as a tragic character. Nothing is actually achieved, but there is always a forlorn hope that something will be. At the same time, the audience knows that because the play is called *Death of a Salesman*, at some point in the drama Willy will die. His interaction with his children at this point, and his use of positive language such as 'Terrific' and 'Good work', enhances the tragedy.

Commentary on Activity 5

1   Although this is a small section of dialogue, much of it is relevant to the wider issues of the play. It references the consumer and credit world which Willy and Linda have become a part of. The appliances, however, are second-rate and do not last very long. The angst and pain this causes Willy is clear to see. He feels there is a conspiracy against the consumer. Linda's speech has a tragic irony because Willy is about to die.

Summary

In this chapter we have examined in some detail one famous modern domestic tragedy, *Death of a Salesman*. You have learnt that when you study a modern domestic tragedy it is essential not only to read the text very closely, but also to think about how wider social issues are explored within the relatively 'tight' world of the characters.

Preparing for the coursework submission

▓ Explains what you need to do to submit your best possible coursework.

This final chapter gives you some hints on writing your AS Level English Literature coursework. These hints are based on the assumption that you have studied the texts and know them well.

One obvious way of preparing for coursework is to use this book. Take each of the chapters in Unit 2 in turn and apply its focus to the actual plays you have been studying. Consider which aspects of tragedy you would like to focus on in each text. A different, but equally important part of preparation involves making the best use of time given to you in class.

▓ What is coursework?

Coursework is different from exams. For exams, you have to prepare for all possibilities. In coursework, you can decide, with your teacher, which particular aspects of the texts you want to focus on. You can only know this, though, when you have read each text in full. Once you have negotiated a task with your teacher, always make sure that you understand fully what is required. After the task has been negotiated and finalised, make sure that you keep to the task – relevance is as important in coursework as in an exam.

Here are some other points to consider, bearing in mind that you will be required to produce a portfolio of two pieces of coursework, each 1,200–1,500 words in length.

▓ You must write separately about two texts, both of them tragedies.

▓ You will probably complete each piece of coursework at a different time in your AS course.

▓ The word limits are important. They are designed for you to write substantially but with sharp focus.

▓ One of the assignments can be **re-creative**. This will be explained later in this chapter.

▓ How much time do you expect to spend on each assignment? How many drafts will you need and how will you amend the first draft? This also will be looked at in more detail later in this chapter.

▓ The marking criteria for coursework are available and can help you understand what you have to do. Ask your teacher for a copy, or follow the link to the AQA website.

Link

See the Introduction to this book for an outline of the full AS requirements.

AQA Examiner's tip

Always make sure that your preparation and writing of coursework is well-focused. Although your coursework will take time to research, plan, shape and eventually write, each stage should lead quickly to the next. Endless tinkering, and endless planning, without actually getting on with the job in hand, can lead to a stale final product.

↻ Types of written coursework

Broadly speaking, there are two types of task which you can work on for this unit. One or both of your responses can be in the more traditional form of the essay, answering a question that has been negotiated with your tutor. There is, though, an alternative option for one of the pieces: this can be a response that is **re-creative**, and so is unlikely to take the form of an essay. If you go for this option, you must also write a **commentary** to go with it. The combined word limit for a creative response and commentary is still 1,200–1,500 words.

The essay

As mentioned above, the essay question you work on will have been negotiated with your teacher. It could focus on one of the aspects of tragedy considered in this unit, or it could ask you more broadly to consider the play as a whole and the extent to which it shows aspects of the tragic genre. Whatever the focus, though, ideally it will ask you to *debate* a proposition rather than just *describe* a feature.

A straightforward task on a Shakespeare play might be something like:

> To what extent is [Character X, e.g. Edmund, Iago, Claudius, Lady Macbeth] presented by Shakespeare as a tragic villain without any redeeming features?

Preparing your task (1)

After the task has been set and you have discussed it with your teacher, get cracking, whatever the deadline might be. Putting the process off, because there is plenty of time, can be fatal. By the time you get round to it, you will have lost momentum and started to forget the text and the task.

Preparing your task (2)

Before you start writing, you will need to organise your thoughts and sort out the references, textual and critical, that will support your ideas. Make sure that the ideas come first, though – otherwise you will tend to take the play chronologically, rather than in the sequence that best suits your argument.

So, for example, as you first think about the task:

> To what extent is [Character X] presented by Shakespeare as a tragic villain without any redeeming features?

you might come up with the following ideas, bearing in mind the word limit you are working to:

- What are some typical characteristics of a tragic villain?
- Character X declares his/her own villainy to the audience – what does he/she claim are the motives for villainy?
- Character X ends the play trying to make some sort of amends.
- Character X seems to enjoy being a villain.
- Character X works via the stupidity of others rather than through direct action.
- Character X potentially has the charisma to appeal to an audience.

In English Literature the best essays confront the task head-on. There is no need to write an introduction that says what you intend to do in your essay – just get on and do it. If you look at the list of points above, clearly any one of them might be a suitable starting point for your argument, depending on the overall line of argument you intend to take.

It is often said, rather loosely, that there is no right answer in English. And when studying a play this can be even more the case, because in addition to the text of the play itself you can consider the possible performances that can come from the text. None the less there are certainly answers that are 'right' in that they argue logically, using suitable evidence to reinforce the points being made.

So how do you decide the best sequence for your ideas? The best way is to try out different sequences in note form, and to draft different openings.

AQA Examiner's tip

Do not follow the play sequentially. The best answers are those that move around the play, referring to whatever part suits the argument as it progresses.

When you find an opening paragraph that clearly leads on to the next ones, you are in business. Then complete your first draft quickly, giving the task your full attention.

How many drafts?

You may want to show your teacher a draft of your work in progress. If so, there are several points to be clear about:

- You cannot expect your teacher to be looking at drafts endlessly: one full draft should be enough, especially if you have used time with your teacher constructively.
- Your teacher can only make general comments, especially if it is a full draft.
- These comments will be about things like structure and reference, both textual and critical.
- Technical accuracy (e.g. in spelling and quotation) is your responsibility.
- Your teacher will make helpful suggestions: it is up to you what you do with these.

Above all, remember that coursework exists to give you the opportunity for independent study. It is your teacher's job to supervise, not to do all the hard work for you.

🔆 Quotation and reference: text of the play

■ Link

See 'Learning to quote and refer' in Chapter 8 (p64).

Earlier in the book, you learned how to quote and refer in the Unit 1 exam. The difference with coursework is that you have more time to research the quotations and references you need. This does not mean, however, that large chunks of the play should now be copied out. Exactly the same rules apply for coursework as for exams:

- You should support your arguments with frequent and relevant textual evidence.
- Quotations should be brief.
- Quotations should be accurate.
- The best quotations are embedded in your own sentences.
- Reference to the text can also help to give evidence: close references can often work better than quotation.
- Quotations and references should never stand alone: they should be used in support of specific points you are making.

Quotation and reference: critical sources

Your coursework essay should present a debate and an argument. To help with this debate you can read the work of critics and then refer to it and/ or quote from it as appropriate. Again, there are some rules to observe:

- Critical comments can help in the shaping of your argument.
- Such comments may support your argument or provide a counter-argument.
- These comments should be tested against the text of the play.
- You should reference the critics by providing the source in your **bibliography** or in endnotes, as described below.

■ Key terms

Bibliography: list of texts you have referred to or quoted from in your work.

As part of your initial preparation for writing coursework, it is worth practising the use of critical sources and comments. Earlier in this unit there was a quotation from the critic Helen Gardner in which she discussed aspects of the character Othello. Here are two examples of the ways you can use a piece of criticism and the original text in your own writing. One is **to quote** directly:

> Although Helen Gardner says of Othello that 'the thing that most sets him apart is his solitariness', there are often moments in the play when he seems to feel very much a part of the society he lives in. Admittedly, he claims that 'Rude am I in my speech/And little blessed with the soft phrase of peace', but here he is putting on a performance for senior politicians.

Another is **to refer** to a critic and the original text:

> Although Helen Gardner believes Othello to be an outsider and a solitary figure, there are often moments in the play when he seems to feel very much a part of the society he lives in. Admittedly, he claims to lack the polished speech of others, but when he says this he is putting on a performance for senior politicians...

💡 Bibliographies and endnotes

Bibliographies are usually listed alphabetically according to the author's surname. Order your entries in the following way: author's surname, author's first name or initial, date of publication, title in italics, place of publication and publisher. For example:

> Bradley, A.C. (1904) *Shakespearean Tragedy*, London: Macmillan.
>
> Miller, Arthur (1987) *Timebends*, London: Methuen.

Alternatively, you may like to use endnotes, where you include a number in the text of your essay, and reference the book at the end of your essay. Here are the same books as above, referenced 1 and 2 in the text of the essay and now including the relevant page numbers:

> 1. Bradley, A.C. (1904) *Shakespearean Tragedy*, London: Macmillan, pp143–4.
>
> 2. Miller, Arthur (1987) *Timebends*, London: Methuen, p191.

■ A re-creative response

In addition to writing an essay, you have the opportunity, if you wish, to write a re-creative response, with commentary.

The word 're-creative' is used because what you are being asked to do in this option is to explore the original text by coming at it from a different angle. A re-creative response is not easier than an essay; it is different, and in the process offers you the chance, if you wish, to have fun by writing in other formats. It is vital, though, that you consult with your teacher if you wish to take this approach.

There are many different tasks that could be devised, depending very much on the plays you are studying. One common aspect of all plays that you study, though, is that they have an ending, and, given that they are tragedies, they usually end with a number of characters dying, while some are left living. Shakespeare frequently gives the last word to a survivor, who reflects on what has happened and apportions out the property and the blame. Arthur Miller, in *Death of a Salesman*, has a whole scene called 'Requiem', in which the actions of the play are reflected on by some of the survivors.

AQA Examiner's tip

In preparing a re-creative response, ask yourself what **critical issues** you are hoping to raise in the process. Make sure that you do more than simply retell the story or copy the style. Indeed, there is little point, for example, in trying to copy Shakespeare's verse/language. Use modern English to make your point, even if you do sometimes echo the language of the original.

> **Activity**
>
> Look at the endings of any tragedies you can access. (Three are included in the extract link.) What is said at the very end of the play?
>
> Now turn to a play you have been studying. In what ways can you reflect on the nature of its ending by either changing it, adding to it, or giving it a fresh context? For example:
>
> - Write a series of other final words spoken by other surviving characters whom we do not hear from at the end.
> - Instead of replacing the final speech, add to it with further responses from characters to the final words, perhaps challenging the final sentiments.
> - Write two 500-word obituaries on characters who have died, or write two 500-word obituaries on one character but in different newspapers, thereby showing potentially different responses to how the character can be perceived.
>
> There is no commentary with this activity.

Link: extracts 8, 9, 10

To complete Activity 1 you may decide to use Hamlet 5.2.370–387, King Lear 5.3.317–325 and Othello 5.2.359–369, which are printed in the Extracts section of this book, extracts 8, 9 and 10.

The commentary

The commentary that accompanies a re-creative piece of writing has two purposes. One is to allow you to discuss what you have been trying to do in terms of re-creating the tragic play. The other, and the more important, is to allow you to reflect on how the re-creative process has thrown light on potential meanings and ambiguities in the play.

How much you write will depend on how much you wrote in the initial re-creative piece. The longer the initial piece, the fewer words you will both need and have available. When planning a re-creative piece, though, do take into account the word limit of the full package. In the third option above, for example, you would have 500 words for your commentary.

Here are some of the things you can address in a commentary, although this is not a complete list:

- why the original play lends itself to the approach you have taken
- the debates and ambiguities in the play that you have attempted to highlight
- further insights you gained into the play through writing this piece
- further ways of approaching the play and/or further ideas you could have explored.

There is no need, though, to dwell on how well you think you have done the exercise. That will be reflected in your mark.

Conclusion

Coursework is included in the assessment of AS Level English Literature so that you can reflect on texts and create individual responses to them. If you work sensibly, it offers the perfect balance to the demands of working under exam conditions.

Extracts

1 Othello 1.2.1-99

Iago. Though in the trade of war I have slain men,
Yet do I hold it very stuff o' the conscience
To do no contriv'd murder: I lack iniquity
Sometimes to do me service. Nine or ten times
I had thought to have yerk'd him here under the ribs.
  Othello. 'Tis better as it is.
  Iago.   Nay, but he prated,
And spoke such scurvy and provoking terms
Against your honour
That, with the little godliness I have,
I did full hard forbear him. But, I pray, sir,
Are you fast married? Be assur'd of this,
That the magnifico is much belov'd,
And hath in his effect a voice potential
As double as the duke's; he will divorce you,
Or put upon you what restraint and grievance
The law—with all his might to enforce it on—
Will give him cable.
  Othello.   Let him do his spite:
My services which I have done the signiory
Shall out-tongue his complaints. 'Tis yet to know,
Which when I know that boasting is an honour
I shall promulgate, I fetch my life and being
From men of royal siege, and my demerits
May speak unbonneted to as proud a fortune
As this that I have reach'd; for know, Iago,
But that I love the gentle Desdemona,
I would not my unhoused free condition
Put into circumscription and confine
For the sea's worth. But, look! what lights come yond?
  Iago. Those are the raised father and his friends:
You were best go in.
  Othello.   Not I; I must be found:
My parts, my title, and my perfect soul
Shall manifest me rightly. Is it they?
  Iago. By Janus, I think no.
  Enter Cassio and certain Officers, with torches.
  Othello. The servants of the duke, and my lieutenant.
The goodness of the night upon you, friends!
What is the news?
  Cassio.   The duke does greet you, general,
And he requires your haste-post-haste appearance,
Even on the instant.
  Othello.   What is the matter, think you?
  Cassio. Something from Cyprus, as I may divine.
It is a business of some heat; the galleys
Have sent a dozen sequent messengers
This very night at one another's heels,
And many of the consuls, rais'd and met,
Are at the duke's already. You have been hotly call'd for;
When, being not at your lodging to be found,
The senate hath sent about three several quests
To search you out.
  Othello.   'Tis well I am found by you.
I will but spend a word here in the house,
And go with you. [*Exit.*
  Cassio.   Ancient, what makes he here?
  Iago. Faith, he to-night hath boarded a land carrack;
If it prove lawful prize, he's made for ever.
  Cassio. I do not understand.
  Iago.   He's married.
  Cassio.   To who?
  Re-enter Othello.
  Iago. Marry, to—Come, captain, will you go?
  Othello.   Have with you.
  Cassio. Here comes another troop to seek for you.
  Iago. It is Brabantio. General, be advis'd;
He comes to bad intent.
*Enter Brabantio, Roderigo, and Officers, with torches
and weapons.*
  Othello.   Holla! stand there!
  Roderigo. Signior, it is the Moor.
  Brabantio.
Down with him, thief! [*They draw on both sides.*
  Iago. You, Roderigo! come, sir, I am for you.
  Othello.
Keep up your bright swords, for the dew will rust them.
Good signior, you shall more command with years
Than with your weapons.
  Brabantio.
O thou foul thief! where hast thou stow'd my daughter?
Damn'd as thou art, thou hast enchanted her;
For I'll refer me to all things of sense,
If she in chains of magic were not bound,
Whether a maid so tender, fair, and happy,
So opposite to marriage that she shunn'd
The wealthy curled darlings of our nation,
Would ever have, to incur a general mock,
Run from her guardage to the sooty bosom
Of such a thing as thou; to fear, not to delight.
Judge me the world, if 'tis not gross in sense
That thou hast practis'd on her with foul charms,
Abus'd her delicate youth with drugs or minerals
That weaken motion: I'll have 't disputed on;

'Tis probable, and palpable to thinking.
I therefore apprehend and do attach thee
For an abuser of the world, a practiser
Of arts inhibited and out of warrant.
Lay hold upon him: if he do resist,
Subdue him at his peril.
  Othello.   Hold your hands,
Both you of my inclining, and the rest:
Were it my cue to fight, I should have known it
Without a prompter. Where will you that I go
To answer this your charge?
  Brabantio.   To prison; till fit time
Of law and course of direct session
Call thee to answer.
  Othello.   What if I do obey?
How may the duke be there with satisfied,
Whose messengers are here about my side,
Upon some present business of the state
To bring me to him?
  Officer.   'Tis true, most worthy signior;
The duke's in council, and your noble self,
I am sure, is sent for.
  Brabantio.   How! the duke in council!
In this time of the night! Bring him away.
Mine's not an idle cause: the duke himself,
Or any of my brothers of the state,
Cannot but feel this wrong as 'twere their own;
For if such actions may have passage free,
Bond-slaves and pagans shall our statesmen be.
[*Exeunt.*

2 Othello 4.1.1-48

Iago. Will you think so?
Othello.   Think so, Iago!
Iago.   What!
To kiss in private?
Othello.   An unauthoriz'd kiss.
Iago. Or to be naked with her friend a-bed
An hour or more, not meaning any harm?
Othello. Naked a-bed, Iago, and not mean harm?
It is hypocrisy against the devil:
They that mean virtuously, and yet do so,
The devil their virtue tempts, and they tempt heaven.
Iago. If they do nothing, 'tis a venial slip;
But if I give my wife a handkerchief,—
Othello. What then?
Iago. Why, then, 'tis hers, my lord; and, being hers,
She may, I think, bestow 't on any man.
Othello. She is protectress of her honour too;
May she give that?
Iago. Her honour is an essence that's not seen;
They have it very oft that have it not:

But for the handkerchief,—
Othello.
By heaven, I would most gladly have forgot it :—
Thou said'st,—O! it comes o'er my memory,
As doth the raven o'er the infected house,
Boding to all,—he had my handkerchief.
  Iago. Ay, what of that?
Othello.   That's not so good now.
  Iago.   What,
If I had said I had seen him do you wrong?
Or heard him say, as knaves be such abroad,
Who having, by their own importunate suit,
Or voluntary dotage of some mistress,
Convinced or supplied them, cannot choose
But they must blab.
Othello.   Hath he said any thing?
Iago. He hath, my lord; but be you well assur'd,
No more than he'll unswear.
Othello.   What hath he said?
Iago. Faith, that he did—I know not what he did.
Othello. What? what?
Iago. Lie—
Othello.   With her?
Iago.   With her, on her; what you will.
Othello. Lie with her! lie on her! We say, lie on her,
When they belie her. Lie with her! that's fulsome.
Handkerchief,—confessions,—handkerchief! To
confess, and be hanged for his labour. First, to be hanged,
and then to confess: I tremble at it. Nature would not
invest herself in such shadowing passion without some
instruction. It is not words that shake me thus. Pish!
Noses, ears, and lips. Is it possible?—Confess!—
Handkerchief!—O devil! [*Falls in a trance.*
  Iago. Work on,
My medicine, work! Thus credulous fools are caught;
And many worthy and chaste dames even thus,
All guiltless, meet reproach. What, ho! my lord!
My lord, I say! Othello!

3 Othello 5.2.54-108

Desdemona. Ay, but not yet to die.
Othello.   Yes, presently;
Therefore confess thee freely of thy sin;
For to deny each article with oath
Cannot remove nor choke the strong conception
That I do groan withal. Thou art to die.
Desdemona. Then Lord have mercy on me!
Othello.   I say, amen.
Desdemona. And have you mercy too! I never did
Offend you in my life; never lov'd Cassio
But with such general warranty of heaven
As I might love; I never gave him token.

Othello. By heaven, I saw my handkerchief in 's hand.
O perjur'd woman! thou dost stone my heart,
And mak'st me call what I intend to do
A murder, which I thought a sacrifice:
I saw the handkerchief.
Desdemona. He found it then;
I never gave it him. Send for him hither;
Let him confess a truth.
Othello. He hath confess'd.
Desdemona. What, my lord?
Othello. That he hath us'd thee.
Desdemona. How? unlawfully?
Othello. Ay.
Desdemona. He will not say so.
Othello. No; his mouth is stopp'd:
Honest Iago hath ta'en order for 't.
Desdemona. O! my fear interprets. What! is he dead?
Othello. Had all his hairs been lives, my great revenge
Had stomach for them all.
Desdemona. Alas! he is betray'd and I undone.
Othello.
Out, strumpet! Weep'st thou for him to my face?
Desdemona. O! banish me, my lord, but kill me not!
Othello. Down, strumpet!
Desdemona. Kill me to-morrow; let me live to-night!
Othello. Nay, if you strive,—
Desdemona. But half an hour!
Othello. Being done, there is no pause.
Desdemona. But while I say one prayer!
Othello. It is too late. [He smothers her.
Emilia. [Within.]
My lord, my lord! what, ho! my lord, my lord!
Othello. What noise is this? Not dead? not yet quite dead?
I that am cruel am yet merciful;
I would not have thee linger in thy pain.
So, so.
Emilia. [Within.] What, ho! my lord, my lord!
Othello. Who's there?
Emilia. [Within.]
O! good my lord, I would speak a word with you!
Othello. Yes; 'tis Emilia: by and by. She's dead.
'Tis like she comes to speak of Cassio's death;
The noise was high. Ha! no more moving?
Still as the grave. Shall she come in? Were 't good?
I think she stirs again: no. What's best to do?
If she come in she'll sure speak to my wife:
My wife! my wife! what wife? I have no wife:
O, insupportable! O heavy hour!
Methinks it should be now a huge eclipse
Of sun and moon, and that the affrighted globe
Should yawn at alteration.
Emilia. [Within.] I do beseech you

That I may speak with you, O! good my lord.
Othello. I had forgot thee: O! come in, Emilia:
Soft, by and by: let me the curtains draw.
Where art thou? [Unlocks the door.

4 Othello 5.2.322-374

Othello. O the pernicious caitiff!
How came you, Cassio, by that handkerchief
That was my wife's?
Cassio. I found it in my chamber;
And he himself confess'd but even now
That there he dropp'd it for a special purpose
Which wrought to his desire.
Othello. O fool! fool! fool!
Cassio. There is besides in Roderigo's letter
How he upbraids Iago that he made him
Brave me upon the watch; whereon it came
That I was cast: and even but now he spake,
After long seeming dead, Iago hurt him,
Iago set him on.
Lodovico.
You must forsake this room and go with us;
Your power and your command is taken off,
And Cassio rules in Cyprus. For this slave,
If there be any cunning cruelty
That can torment him much and hold him long,
It shall be his. You shall close prisoner rest.
Till that the nature of your fault be known
To the Venetian state. Come, bring him away.
Othello. Soft you; a word or two before you go.
I have done the state some service, and they know 't;
No more of that. I pray you, in your letters,
When you shall these unlucky deeds relate,
Speak of me as I am; nothing extenuate,
Nor set down aught in malice: then, must you speak
Of one that lov'd not wisely but too well;
Of one not easily jealous, but, being wrought,
Perplex'd in the extreme; of one whose hand,
Like the base Indian, threw a pearl away
Richer than all his tribe; of one whose subdu'd eyes
Albeit unused to the melting mood,
Drop tears as fast as the Arabian trees
Their med'cinable gum. Set you down this;
And say besides, that in Aleppo once,
Where a malignant and a turban'd Turk
Beat a Venetian and traduc'd the state,
I took by the throat the circumcised dog,
And smote him thus. [Stabs himself.
Lodovico. O bloody period!
Gratiano. All that's spoke is marr'd.
Othello. I kiss'd thee ere I kill'd thee; no way but this,
[Falling upon Desdemona.

Killing myself to die upon a kiss. [Dies.
Cassio. This did I fear, but thought he had no weapon;
For he was great of heart.
Lodovico.   [To Iago.] O Spartan dog!
More fell than anguish, hunger, or the sea.
Look on the tragic loading of this bed;
This is thy work; the object poisons sight;
Let it be hid. Gratiano, keep the house,
And seize upon the fortunes of the Moor,
For they succeed on you. To you, lord governor,
Remains the censure of this hellish villain,
The time, the place, the torture; O! enforce it.
Myself will straight aboard, and to the state
This heavy act with heavy heart relate. [Exeunt.

5 Titus Andronicus 3.1.150-246

Aaron. Titus Andronicus, my lord the emperor
Sends thee this word: that, if thou love thy sons,
Let Marcus, Lucius, or thyself, old Titus,
Or any one of you, chop off your hand,
And send it to the king: he for the same
Will send thee hither both thy sons alive;
And that shall be the ransom for their fault.
Titus. O gracious emperor! O gentle Aaron!
Did ever raven sing so like a lark,
That gives sweet tidings of the sun's uprise?
With all my heart, I'll send the emperor my hand:
Good Aaron, wilt thou help to chop it off?
Lucuis. Stay, father! for that noble hand of thine,
That hath thrown down so many enemies,
Shall not be sent; my hand will serve the turn:
My youth can better spare my blood than you;
And therefore mine shall save my brothers' lives.
Marcus.
Which of your hands hath not defended Rome,
And rear'd aloft the bloody battle-axe,
Writing destruction on the enemy's castle?
O! none of both but are of high desert:
My hand hath been but idle; let it serve
To ransom my two nephews from their death;
Then have I kept it to a worthy end.
Aaron. Nay, come, agree whose hand shall go along,
For fear they die before their pardon come.
Marcus. My hand shall go.
Lucuis.   By heaven, it shall not go!
Titus. Sirs, strive no more: such wither'd herbs as these
Are meet for plucking up, and therefore mine.
Lucuis. Sweet father, if I shall be thought thy son,
Let me redeem my brothers both from death.
Marcus. And for our father's sake, and mother's care,
Now let me show a brother's love to thee.
Tilt. Agree between you; I will spare my hand.

Lucuis. Then I'll go fetch an axe.
Marcus.   But I will use the axe.
[Exeunt Lucius and Marcus.
Titus. Come hither, Aaron; I'll deceive them both:
Lend me thy hand, and I will give thee mine.
Aaron. [Aside.] If that be call'd deceit, I will be honest,
And never, whilst I live, deceive men so:
But I'll deceive you in another sort,
And that you'll say, ere half an hour pass.
[Cuts off Titus' hand.
Re-enter Lucius and Marcus.
Titus. Now stay your strife: what shall be is dispatch'd.
Good Aaron, give his majesty my hand:
Tell him it was a hand that warded him
From thousand dangers; bid him bury it;
More hath it merited; that let it have.
As for my sons, say I account of them
As jewels purchas'd at an easy price;
And yet dear too, because I bought mine own.
Aaron. I go, Andronicus; and for thy hand,
Look by and by to have thy sons with thee.
[Aside.] Their heads, I mean. O! how this villany
Doth fat me with the very thoughts of it.
Let fools do good, and fair men call for grace,
Aaron will have his soul black like his face. [Exit.
Titus. O! here I lift this one hand up to heaven,
And bow this feeble ruin to the earth:
If any power pities wretched tears,
To that I call! [To Lavinia.]
What! wilt thou kneel with me?
Do, then, dear heart; for heaven shall hear our prayers,
Or with our sighs we'll breathe the welkin dim,
And stain the sun with fog, as sometime clouds
When they do hug him in their melting bosoms.
Marcus. O! brother, speak with possibilities,
And do not break into these deep extremes.
Titus. Is not my sorrow deep, having no bottom?
Then be my passions bottomless with them.
Marcus. But yet let reason govern thy lament.
Titus. If there were reason for these miseries,
Then into limits could I bind my woes.
When heaven doth weep, doth not the earth o'erflow?
If the winds rage, doth not the sea wax mad,
Threat'ning the welkin with his big-swoln face?
And wilt thou have a reason for this coil?
I am the sea; hark! how her sighs do blow;
She is the weeping welkin, I the earth:
Then must my sea be moved with her sighs;
Then must my earth with her continual tears
Become a deluge, overflow'd and drown'd;
For why my bowels cannot hide her woes,
But like a drunkard must I vomit them.
Then give me leave, for losers will have leave

To ease their stomachs with their bitter tongues.
Enter a Messenger, with two heads and a hand.
Messenger. Worthy Andronicus, ill art thou repaid
For that good hand thou sent'st the emperor.
Here are the heads of thy two noble sons,
And here's thy hand, in scorn to thee sent back:
Thy griefs their sports, thy resolution mock'd;
That woe is me to think upon thy woes,
More than remembrance of my father's death. [*Exit.*
  Marcus. Now let hot Ætna cool in Sicily,
And be my heart an ever burning hell!
These miseries are more than may be borne.
To weep with them that weep doth ease some deal,
But sorrow flouted at is double death.

6 Titus Andronicus 5.3.1-93

Lucius. Uncle Marcus, since it is my father's mind
That I repair to Rome, I am content.
  First Goth. And ours with thine, befall what fortune
will.
  Lucius. Good uncle, take you in this barbarous Moor,
This ravenous tiger, this accursed devil;
Let him receive no sustenance, fetter him,
Till he be brought unto the empress' face,
For testimony of her foul proceedings:
And see the ambush of our friends be strong;
I fear the emperor means no good to us.
  Aaron. Some devil whisper curses in mine ear,
And prompt me, that my tongue may utter forth
The venomous malice of my swelling heart!
  Lucius. Away, inhuman dog! unhallow'd slave!
Sirs, help our uncle to convey him in.
[Exeunt Goths, with AARON. Trumpets sound.
The trumpets show the emperor is at hand.
    Enter Saturninus and Tamora, with Æmilius,
Senators, Tribunes, and Others.
  Saturnius. What! hath the firmament more suns than
one?
  Lucius. What boots it thee, to call thyself a sun?
  Marcus. Rome's emperor, and nephew, break the parle;
These quarrels must be quietly debated.
The feast is ready which the careful Titus
Hath ordain'd to an honourable end,
For peace, for love, for league, and good to Rome:
Please you, therefore, draw nigh, and take your places.
  Saturnius. Marcus, we will. [*Hautboys sound.*
  *Enter Titus, dressed like a cook, Lavinia, veiled, young
Lucius, and Others. Titus places the dishes on the table.*
  Titus. Welcome, my gracious lord; welcome, dread
queen;
Welcome, ye war-like Goths; welcome, Lucius;
And welcome, all. Although the cheer be poor,

'Twill fill your stomachs; please you eat of it.
  Saturnius. Why art thou thus attir'd, Andronicus?
  Titus. Because I would be sure to have all well
To entertain your highness, and your empress.
  Tamora. We are beholding to you, good Andronicus.
  Titus. An if your highness knew my heart, you were.
My lord the emperor, resolve me this:
Was it well done of rash Virginius
To slay his daughter with his own right hand,
Because she was enforced, stain'd, and deflower'd?
  Saturnius. It was, Andronicus.
  Titus. Your reason, mighty lord?
  Saturnius. Because the girl should not survive her
shame,
And by her presence still renew his sorrows.
  Titus. A reason mighty, strong, and effectual;
A pattern, precedent, and lively warrant,
For me most wretched, to perform the like.
Die, die, Lavinia, and thy shame with thee;
And with thy shame thy father's sorrow die!
[Kills Lavinia.
  Saturnius. What hast thou done, unnatural and
unkind?
  Titus. Kill'd her, for whom my tears have made me
blind.
I am as woeful as Virginius was,
And have a thousand times more cause than he
To do this outrage: and it is now done.
  Saturnius. What! was she ravish'd? tell who did the
deed.
  Titus. Will't please you eat? will't please your highness
feed?
  Tamora. Why hast thou slain thine only daughter thus?
  Titus. Not I; 'twas Chiron and Demetrius:
They ravish'd her, and cut away her tongue:
And they, 'twas they, that did her all this wrong.
  Saturnius. Go fetch them hither to us presently.
  Titus. Why, there they are both, baked in that pie;
Whereof their mother daintily hath fed,
Eating the flesh that she herself hath bred.
'Tis true, 'tis true; witness my knife's sharp point.
[Kills Tamora.
  Saturnius. Die, frantic wretch, for this accursed deed!
[Kills Titus.
  Lucius. Can the son's eye behold his father bleed?
There's meed for meed, death for a deadly deed!
*[Kills Saturninus. A great tumult. The people in
confusion*
disperse. Marcus, Lucius, and their partisans, go up into
the balcony.
  Marcus. You sad-fac'd men, people and sons of Rome,
By uproar sever'd, like a flight of fowl
Scatter'd by winds and high tempestuous gusts,
O! let me teach you how to knit again

This scatter'd corn into one mutual sheaf,
These broken limbs again into one body;
Lest Rome herself be bane unto herself,
And she whom mighty kingdoms curtsy to,
Like a forlorn and desperate castaway,
Do shameful execution on herself.
But if my frosty signs and chaps of age,
Grave witnesses of true experience,
Cannot induce you to attend my words,
[To Lucius.]
Speak, Rome's dear friend, as erst our ancestor,
When with his solemn tongue he did discourse
To love-sick Dido's sad attending ear
The story of that baleful burning night
When subtle Greeks surpris'd King Priam's Troy;
Tell us what Sinon hath bewitch'd our ears,
Or who hath brought the fatal engine in
That gives our Troy, our Rome, the civil wound.
My heart is not compact of flint nor steel,
Nor can I utter all our bitter grief,
But floods of tears will drown my oratory,
And break my very utterance, even in the time
When it should move you to attend me most,
Lending your kind commiseration.

7 King Lear 1.1.35-91

Lear. Meantime we shall express our darker purpose.
Give me the map there. Know that we have divided
In three our kingdom; and 'tis our fast intent
To shake all cares and business from our age,
Conferring them on younger strengths, while we
Unburden'd crawl toward death. Our son of Cornwall,
And you, our no less loving son of Albay,
We have this hour a constant will to publish
Our daughters' several dowers, that future strife
May be prevented now. The princes, France and
Burgundy,
Great rivals in our youngest daughter's love,
Long in our court have made their amorous sojourn,
And here are to be answer'd. Tell me, my daughters,—
Since now we will divest us both of rule,
Interest of territory, cares of state,—
Which of you shall we say doth love us most?
That we our largest bounty may extend
Where nature doth with merit challenge. Goneril,
Our eldest-born, speak first.
  Goneril.
Sir, I love you more than words can wield the matter;
Dearer than eye-sight, space, and liberty;
Beyond what can be valu'd, rich or rare;
No less than life, with grace, health, beauty, honour;
As much as child e'er lov'd, or father found;

A love that makes breath poor and speech unable;
Beyond all manner of so much I love you.
  Cordelia. [Aside.]
What shall Cordelia do? Love, and be silent.
  Lear. Of all these bounds, even from this line to this,
With shadowy forests and with champains rich'd,
With plenteous rivers and wide-skirted meads,
We make thee lady: to thine and Albany's issue
Be this perpetual. What says our second daughter,
Our dearest Regan, wife to Cornwall? Speak.
  Regan. I am made of that self metal as my sister,
And prize me at her worth. In my true heart
I find she names my very deed of love;
Only she comes too short: that I profess
Myself an enemy to all other joys
Which the most precious square of sense possesses
And find I am alone felicitate
In your dear highness' love.
  Cordelia. [Aside.] Then, poor Cordelia!
And yet not so; since, I am sure, my love's
More richer than my tongue.
  Lear. To thee and thine, hereditary ever,
Remain this ample third of our fair kingdom,
No less in space, validity, and pleasure,
Than that conferr'd on Goneril. Now, our joy,
Although our last, not least; to whose young love
The vines of France and milk of Burgundy
Strive to be interess'd; what can you say to draw
A third more opulent than your sisters? Speak.
  Cordelia. Nothing, my lord.
  Lear. Nothing?
  Cordelia. Nothing.
  Lear. Nothing will come of nothing: speak again.
  Cordelia. Unhappy that I am, I cannot heave
My heart into my mouth: I love your majesty
According to my bond; nor more nor less.

8 Hamlet 5.2.370-387

Fortinbras. Let us haste to hear it,
And call the noblest to the audience.
For me, with sorrow I embrace my fortune;
I have some rights of memory in this kingdom,
Which now to claim my vantage doth invite me.
  Horatio. Of that I shall have also cause to speak,
And from his mouth whose voice will draw on more:
But let this same be presently perform'd,
Even while men's minds are wild, lest more mischance
On plots and errors happen.
Fortinbras. Let four captains
Bear Hamlet, like a soldier, to the stage;
For he was likely, had he been put on,
To have prov'd most royally: and, for his passage,

The soldiers' music and the rites of war
Speak loudly for him.
Take up the bodies: such a sight as this
Becomes the field, but here shows much amiss.
Go, bid the soldiers shoot. [A dead march.
Exeunt, bearing off the bodies; after which a peal of
ordnance is shot off.

9 King Lear 5.3.317-325

Albany. Bear them from hence. Our present business
Is general woe. [To Kent and Edgar.]
Friends of my soul, you twain
Rule in this realm, and the gor'd state sustain.
 Kent. I have a journey, sir, shortly to go;
My master calls me, I must not say no.
 Albany. The weight of this sad time we must obey;
Speak what we feel, not what we ought to say.
The oldest hath borne most: we that are young,
Shall never see so much, nor live so long.
[Exeunt, with a dead march.

10 Othello 5.2.359-369

Lodovico.　　　[To Iago.] O Spartan dog!
More fell than anguish, hunger, or the sea.
Look on the tragic loading of this bed;
This is thy work; the object poisons sight;
Let it be hid. Gratiano, keep the house,
And seize upon the fortunes of the Moor,
For they succeed on you. To you, lord governor,
Remains the censure of this hellish villain,
The time, the place, the torture; O! enforce it.
Myself will straight aboard, and to the state
This heavy act with heavy heart relate. [Exeunt.

11 Hedda Gabler Act 1

Tesman. But, Aunt Juju, take a good look at Hedda before
you go. Isn't she pretty and charming?
Miss Tesman. Dear boy, there's nothing new in that.
Hedda's been a beauty ever since the day she was born.
(Nods and goes right)
Tesman. *(follows her)* Yes, but have you noticed how
strong and healthy she's looking? And how she's filled
out since we went away?
Miss Tesman. *(stops and turns)* Filled out?
Hedda *(walks across the room).* Oh, can't we forget it?
Tesman. Yes, Aunt Juju – you can't see it so clearly with
that dress on. But I've good reason to know –
Hedda *(by the French windows, impatiently).* You
haven't good reason to know anything.
Tesman. It must have been the mountain air up there in
the Tyrol –
Hedda *(curtly, interrupts him).* I'm exactly the same as
when I went away.
Tesman. You keep on saying so. But you're not. I'm right
aren't I, Auntie Juju?
Miss Tesman *(has folded her hands and is gazing at her).*
She's beautiful – beautiful. Hedda is beautiful. *(Goes
over to hedda, takes her head between her hands, draws
it down and kisses her hair.)* God bless and keep you,
Hedda Tesman. For George's sake.
Hedda *(frees herself, politely).* Oh – let me go please.
Miss Tesman *(quietly, emotionally).* I shall come and see
you both every day.
Tesman. Yes Auntie Juju, please do. What?
Miss Tesman. Good-bye! Good-bye!
She goes out into the hall. Tesman follows her. The
door remains open. Tesman is heard sending his love to
Aunt Rena and thanking Miss Tesman for his slippers.
Meanwhile Hedda walks up and down the room,
raising her arms and clenching her fists as though in
desperation. Then she throws aside the curtains from
the French windows and stands there, looking out. A
few moments later, Tesman returns and closes the door
behind him.
Tesman *(picks up his slippers from the floor).* What are
you looking at, Hedda?
Hedda *(calm and controlled again).* Only the leaves.
They're so golden and withered.
Tesman *(wraps up the slippers and lays them on the
table).* Well, we're in September now.
Hedda **(***restless again).* Yes. We're already into September.
Tesman. Auntie Juju was behaving rather oddly, I
thought, didn't you? Almost as though she was in church
or something. I wonder what came over her. Any idea?
Hedda. I hardly know her. Does she often act like that?
Tesman. Not to the extent she did today.
Hedda *(goes away from the French windows).* Do you
think she was hurt by what I said about the hat?
Tesman. Oh, I don't think so. A little at first, perhaps –
Hedda. But what a thing to do, throw her hat in
someone's drawing-room. People don't do such things.
Tesman. I'm sure Auntie Juju doesn't do it very often.
Hedda. Oh well, I'll make it up with her.
Tesman. Oh Hedda, would you?
Hedda. When you see them this afternoon invite her to
come out here this evening.
Tesman. You bet I will! I say, there's another thing which
would please her enormously.
Hedda. Oh?
Tesman. If you could bring yourself to call her Auntie
Juju. For my sake, Hedda? What?
Hedda. Oh no, really, Tesman, you mustn't ask me to do
that. I've told you so once before. I'll try to call her Aunt
Juliana. That's as far as I'll go.
Tesman *(after a moment).* I say, Hedda, is anything
wrong? What?

Hedda. I'm just looking at my old piano. It doesn't really go with all this.

Tesman. As soon as I start getting my salary we'll see about changing it.

Hedda. No, no, don't let's change it. I don't want to part with it. We can move it into that little room and get another one to put in here.

Tesman (a little downcast). Yes, we – might do that.

Hedda (picks up the bunch of flowers from the piano). These flowers weren;t here when we arrived last night.

Tesman. I expect Auntie Juju brought them.

Hedda. Here's a card. *(Takes it out and reads.)* 'Will come back later today.' Guess who it's from?

Tesman. No idea. Who? What?

Hedda. It says: 'Mrs Elvsted.'

Tesman. No, really? Mrs Elvsted! She used to be Miss Rysing didn't she?

Hedda. Yes. She was the one with that irritating hair she was always showing off. I hear she used to be an old flame of yours.

Tesman (laughs). The didn't last long. Anyway, that was before I got to know you, Hedda. By Jove, fancy her being in town.

Hedda. Strange that she should call. I only knew her at school.

Tesman. Yes, I haven't seen her for – oh, heaven knows how long. I don't know how she manages to stick it out up there in the north. What?

Hedda (thinks for a moment, then says suddenly). Tell me, Tesman, doesn't he live somewhere up in those parts? You know – Eilert Loevborg?

Tesman. Yes, that's right. So he does.

Bertha enters from the hall.

Bertha. She's here again, madam. The lady who came and left the flowers. *(Points.)* The ones you're holding.

Hedda. Oh, is she? Well, show her in.

Bertha opens the door for Mrs Elvsted and goes out. Mrs Elvsted is a delicately built woman with gentle, attractive features. Her eyes are light blue, large, and somewhat prominent, with a frightened, questioning expression. Her hair is extremely fair, almost flaxen, and is exceptionally wavy and abundant. She is two or three years younger than Hedda. She is wearing a dark visiting dress, in good taste but not quite in the latest fashion. (Goes cordially to greet her.) Dear Mrs Elvsted, good morning! How delightful to see you again after all this time!

Mrs Elvsted (nervously, trying to control herself). Yes, it's many years since we met.

Tesman. And since we met. What?

Hedda. Thank you for your lovely flowers.

Mrs Elvsted. I wanted to come yesterday afternoon. But they told me you were away-

Tesman. You've only just arrived in town, then> What?

Mrs Elvsted. I got here yesterday, around midday. Oh, I became almost desperate when I heard you weren't here.

Hedda. Desperate> Why?

Tesman. My dear Mrs Rysing – Elvsted –

Hedda. There's nothing wrong, I hope?

Mrs Elvsted. Yes, there is. And I don't know anyone else here whom I can turn to.

Hedda (puts the flowers down on the table). Come and sit with me on the sofa -

12 The Patriot

An Old Story

It was roses, roses, all the way,
With myrtle mixed in my path like mad;
The house-roofs seemed to heave and sway,
The church-spires flamed, such flags they had,
A year ago on this very day.

The air broke into a mist with bells,
The old walls rocked with the crowd and cries.
Had I said, 'Good folk, mere noise repels--
But give me your sun from yonder skies!'
They had answered 'And afterward, what else?'

Alack, it was I who leaped at the sun
To give it my loving friends to keep!
Naught man could do, have I left undone:
And you see my harvest, what I reap
This very day, now a year is run.

There's nobody on the house-tops now--
Just a palsied few at the windows set;
For the best of the sight is, all allow,
At the Shambles' Gate--or, better yet,
By the very scaffold's foot, I trow.

I go in the rain, and, more than needs,
A rope cuts both my wrists behind;
And I think, by the feel, my forehead bleeds,
For they fling, whoever has a mind,
Stones at me for my year's misdeeds.

Thus I entered, and thus I go!
In triumphs, people have dropped down dead,
'Paid by the world, what dost thou owe
Me?'--God might question; now instead,
'Tis God shall repay: I am safer so.

by Robert Browning

Glossary

A

abdicate: to renounce or give up a throne.

absence: something that is missing from a text, but whose absence can be seen to be significant.

alienation: a feeling that people experience when the world around them becomes unfamiliar and disorientating.

anti-hero: a character who does not fit the normal model of heroism.

aside: a very brief soliloquy within a normal sequence of dialogue, in which a character speaks a short line specifically to the audience, telling their true thoughts about events on stage.

attributed: describes direct speech that is identified, i.e. the reader is told who is speaking.

B

bibliography: list of texts you have referred to or quoted from in your work.

blank verse: (see verse)

box set: a realistic 3-dimensional set, with the fourth wall cut so the audience can see in.

C

catharsis: purification of mind and body brought about by the release of emotions

chaos: inversion of the normal order in a society. In some tragedies the central character breaks down; in others the whole of society disintegrates, while in several both the characters and the society fall apart and collapse. Chaos usually leads to death.

characterisation: the way in which an author creates and uses characters, and why.

chronological order: the sequence of events as they happen, in a time line that goes from A, the start of events, to say E, the end.

classical: usually refers to literature written in ancient Greece or Rome.

climax: the point of highest dramatic tension or a major turning point in the action of a play.

commentary: a piece of writing in which you discuss your literary choices and reflect on how the re-creative process has increased your understanding of the play.

complication: a situation or a detail of character which complicates the plot.

consumerism: contemporary society's obsession with consumer spending on new products and services.

contemporary: refers to plays written in the late twentieth or twenty-first centuries.

context: the circumstances surrounding a text (e.g. where it first appeared, social attitudes today) which affect the way it is understood. **contexts of production:** circumstances that might affect a text at the time of its writing. **contexts of reception:** circumstances that might affect a text at the time of its being read.

conventions: the accepted rules, structures and customs we expect to see in a specific genre of writing.

critical issues: ideas suggested by literary critics. A range of other readers' opinions can help you to reach your own view of the play.

cultural stereotype: used here to suggest that authors present characters with features which we are conditioned to recognise as having a certain meaning. Bright eyes, for example, will often suggest wisdom and creativity.

D

death: the outcome of chaos/ disorder in a tragedy.

dialect: regional and sometimes social variations in language.

direct speech: the actual words spoken by characters in a narrative.

disorder: inversion of the normal order in a society.

domestic: refers to drama set in a household. It is does not have a grand or ambitious theme.

drama: published texts, improvisation and workshop activity.

dramatis personæ: the list of characters in a play, found at the start of the script.

dumb-show: a dramatic convention of the period whereby a story is told in silent action or mime.

duplicity: deceitful behaviour.

E

empathise: to identify with someone else's feelings or experiences.

epic: refers to a literature which has a grand or ambitious theme.

establishment: refers to how texts begin, the work the author does for the reader at the beginning of the text. Establishment can involve introducing people, places, time, etc.

eye dialect: the representation of the vocabulary, grammar and sound of dialect in ordinary letters, in contrast to the phonetic representation (with special symbols) that a linguist would use.

F

feminism: recognition of the historical and cultural subordination of women, and the resolve to do something about it.

first-person narrative: a story told through the voice of one of the characters, using 'I'.

form: the aspects of a text in its totality that enable it to be identified as a novel, or a poem, or an epistolary novel (i.e. a story told in the form of letters) or a sonnet (a poem of 14 lines), etc.

free: in a technical sense, describes thought or speech that is not attributed, i.e. the reader is not told specifically who is speaking or thinking.

G

genre: a type of text (e.g. a crime novel, a narrative poem).

H

hamartia: error committed by a tragic hero or heroine which leads to their downfall

hubris: excessive pride or self-confidence which leads a tragic character to commit hamartia

I

iambic pentameter: (see verse)

ideology: the attitudes, values and assumptions that the text contains, and which readers are expected to share - although they don't actually have to.

illegitimate: born of parents who are not married to each other.

imitation: in Aristotle's theory, the realistic representation in drama.

indirect speech: speech that is reported by the narrator, giving a version of the words spoken rather than the words themselves.

inevitability: refers to events which cannot be prevented. They are certain to happen.

integrity: A person's self-worth and honesty.

irony: saying something in such a way as to convey a different meaning, usually the opposite

L

language: in this context, generally refers to specific words or phrases in the text.

M

magnitude: great importance or seriousness.

materialism: an excessive regard for material possessions.

metaphor: involves the transfer of meaning, with one thing described as another. When one thing is described as being *like* another it is known as **simile**.

modern: most often refers to plays written in the late nineteenth or twentieth century.

mythology: a traditional tale or belief.

N

narrative: involves how the events and causes are shown, and the various methods used to do this showing.

necromancer: Someone who predicts things by communicating with the dead.

noble: describes someone who possesses excellent qualities of mind and character and who is not mean or petty.

O

oligarchy: a form of government in which the power is in the hands of an individual or a small group. An **oligarch** is a member or supporter of an oligarchy, for example, King Lear is an oligarch at the start of the play.

P

pageantry: a public show or procession, sometimes involving people in elaborate costume.

patriarchal society: a society whose ideology and mechanisms of control are in the power of men and not women.

play-within-the-play: a short play, sometimes a dumb-show, presented in the course of the main action.

plot: the chain of causes and circumstances which connect the various events and places into some sort of relationship with each other.

predictive: allowing the audience to predict what will happen to the characters. Writers do this by inserting **signifiers**, or pointers, into the text to 'set up' the circumstances of a drama.

procrastination: to postpone or put off doing something.

prose: 'normal' speech in paragraphs and not poetry.

pun: a play on words for comic effect.

R

readers: other people who have commented upon or have considered the tragedies we are reading. They may be academics, directors, journalists, reviewers or members of the audience.

re-creative response: a piece of writing which throws light on the original text in a creative rather than analytical way.

redemption: making up for one's faults, or being saved from the consequences of one's earlier actions.

regicide: the killing of a king

Renaissance: period of European history, approximately from 1550 to 1660.

resolution: the point at which the chief dramatic **complication** is worked out, signalling the dawn of a new period of time in the imagined world of the play, where hopefully the same mistakes will not be made.

revelation: the offering of information to the audience about characters and their situations.

rhetoric: the art of using words impressively.

S

semiotics: relates to the meanings of signs

sensationalism: use of events, actions, etc. that cause great excitement or scandal.

setting: the location where the tragedy takes place.

signifiers: signs or symbols used in dramatic texts as pointers to the direction of the drama and its meanings.

simile: a comparison where the comparison is explicitly made by using words such as 'like' or 'as'.

soliloquy: a speech spoken by a character, who is usually alone on the stage, in which they tell or confess their thoughts to the audience.

speaker: the person whose voice is heard in a poem, as opposed to the author.

speech marks: inverted commas used to indicate the start and end of direct speech.

story: all the various events that are going to be shown.

structure: how the significant parts of a text work together to form a whole, e.g. the connection between chapters in a novel.

sub-genre: a genre which breaks off from an existing genre to become a new one.

sub-plot: a secondary plot which parallels events of the main plot of a drama (or novel).

subvert: To overthrow and to turn established order upside-down.

suffering: the pain or distress that the characters must endure in a tragedy.

symbol: something that stands for something else. In literary texts, the connection is usually not directly stated and the reader is expected to recognise the symbol for what it represents.

symbolic: involves the reader making meanings and connections that are not directly stated (in contrast to **metaphor**, defined below).

T

third-person narrative: a story told through the voice of a narrator who is not one of the characters in the story.

three unities: these are action, time and place. If a play observes the three unities it will feature action that is sequential, takes place in one day and in one specific place.

V

verse: rhymed or (most usually) unrhymed poetry that is found in Shakespearean and other drama of the period. The unrhymed form is written in **iambic pentameters** (ten-syllable lines with five stresses) and when performed, closely imitates the rhythm of speech in English. It is sometimes called **blank verse**.

W

well-made play: a play which is tightly constructed and in which all loose ends of the plot are tied up at the end.

Index

M

McEwan, Ian, *Enduring Love* 25–6, 27, 39–41
Madden, Matt, *99 Ways to Tell a Story* 47–9, 53–4
magnitude 83, 87
Marlowe, Christopher, *Dr Faustus* 95, 98–102, 107
meaningful absence 20
metaphor 3, 11, 46
Miller, Arthur 68, 99
  Death of a Salesman 115–121
modern tragedy 68, 114–121

N

names, characterisation 29–30
narrative, aspects of 1–73
narrator 36, 37, 41, 47–8
Newman, Karen 79–80, 85
noble heroes 72
notes 2, 3
novels
  characterisation 31–2
  examination vi
  notes 2
  reading 1–2
  studying 1–2
  thought 39–41
  time 20, 22–3

O

O'Casey, Sean, *The Shadow of a Gunman* 120
O'Neill, Eugene 78, 109
  Long Day's Journey into Night 120
order 95–102

P

pageantry 93
pentameters 76
place 6, 9–18, 58, 85–6
play-within-the-play 95
plot, definition 4
poetry
  characterisation 30–1
  examination vi
  places 9–13
  points of view 52–4
  reading 2–3
  studying 2–3
  thought 39
  time 20–2
  voices 43–5
points of view 7–8, 46–54, 58–9
predictive 74
prose fiction, place 13–18
proximity to the action 48–50

Q

quotations 3, 64–5, 98, 124–5

R

Ravenscroft, Edward 92
re-creative response vii, 125–6
  ideas for 73, 87, 93, 101, 121
  points of view 52
  preparing for submission 122
reading 1–3, 66
real-life events, tragedy 70, 71–3
reference 64–5, 124–5
Renaissance 82, 88, 100
representation 5, 9, 29
resolution 78
revenge 88–94, 95
revision 63
rhetoric 93
rhyme 3
rhythm 3
Romeo and Juliet (film 1997) 70
Rossetti, Christina, *Sister Maude* 52, 54

S

scenes 6, 9–18
science fiction 13
semiotics 51
Seneca 88
sensationalism 93
sequence 6–7, 19–28, 58
Shakespeare, William vi
  classical tragedy 68
  Hamlet: Prince of Denmark 90, 95–8, 101, 107
  Henry V 100
  King Lear 85, 103–13
  Macbeth 85, 86
  Othello 74–82, 85, 86–7
  Richard III 99
  Romeo and Juliet 70, 85
  three unities 86
  Titus Andronicus 88–94
Shelley, Mary, *Frankenstein* 24
shifting perspectives 50–1
signifiers 72, 74
soliloquys 75, 94–5
speakers 8
speech 36–7, 38–9
speech marks 38
Stanislavski, Konstantin 109
Star Wars films 70, 85
story, definition 4
storytelling 4
Strindberg, August 68
  The Father 120
structure viii, 3
sub-genre 19

T

sub-plots 107, 110
suffering 68, 86
symbols 11, 75

television programmes, tragedy 69
Tennyson, Alfred, Lord, *Godiva* 24, 44
third-person narrative 7, 41, 47–8
Thomas, Edward 13
thought 39–43, 47, 83
three unities 85–6
time 6–7, 19–28, 58, 85–6, 117
time, unity of 85–6
time frames 23–4
Titanic (film 1997) 69
Tolkien, J.R.R., *Lord of the Rings* 70, 85
tragedy 66–126
tragic flaw 85, 86
tragic hero 72, 74–5, 78
  Aristotle 83–4, 86
  revenge 90–92
  Shakespeare's *Titus Andronicus* 88
  as villains 99
tragic victims 74, 76, 78, 95
tragic villains 74, 75–6, 78
Tristan & Isolde (film 2006) 70
Tyler, Anne, *Digging to America* 22–3, 41–3

U

understanding 78
Unit 1 vi, 1–65
Unit 2 vi–vii, 66–126
unities 85–6

V

verse, drama 76
victims 74, 76, 78
Victorian poetry 60
villains 74, 75–6, 78, 99
violence 88–94
voices 3, 7, 36–45, 58

W

Waters, Sarah, *Fingersmith* 13–14
Wells, Stanley 92, 93
Wertenbaker, Timberlake 68
Williams, Tennessee 105
  Cat on a Hot Tin Roof 120
Woman's Own 71–73
writing vii, 63–4
  see also essays; re-creative response